SPEAKING WITH A PURPOSE

SPEAKING WITH A PURPOSE

ARTHUR KOCH

Milwaukee Area Technical College

PRENTICE HALL, Englewood Cliffs, New Jersey 07632

Library of Congress Cataloging-in-Publication Data

KOCH, ARTHUR, (date)
    Speaking with a purpose.

    Includes index.
    1. Public speaking. I. Title.
PN4121.K917 1988   808.5'1   87-11370
ISBN 0-13-825878-3

Editorial/production supervision
and interior design: Robert DeGeorge
Cover design: Wanda Lubelska
Manufacturing buyer: Harry P. Baisley

For My Mother

© 1988 by Prentice Hall
A Division of Simon & Schuster
Englewood Cliffs, New Jersey 07632

Printed in the United States of America

10 9 8 7 6 5 4 3 2

ISBN 0-13-825878-3 01

PRENTICE-HALL INTERNATIONAL (UK) LIMITED, *London*
PRENTICE-HALL OF AUSTRALIA PTY. LIMITED, *Sydney*
PRENTICE-HALL CANADA INC., *Toronto*
PRENTICE-HALL HISPANOAMERICANA, S.A., *Mexico*
PRENTICE-HALL OF INDIA PRIVATE LIMITED, *New Delhi*
PRENTICE-HALL OF JAPAN, INC., *Tokyo*
PRENTICE-HALL OF SOUTHEAST ASIA PTE. LTD., *Singapore*
EDITORA PRENTICE-HALL DO BRASIL, LTDA., *Rio de Janeiro*

CONTENTS

PREFACE

Speaking with a Purpose is a brief introduction to speechmaking, based primarily on a traditional public-speaking approach. It is designed to aid beginning speakers in developing the skills they need to prepare and deliver effective speeches.

There are a multitude of benefits for the person who can communicate successfully through speech. Improved self-concept, increased confidence, greater employability, and the ability to get along better with others are just a few of these benefits.

After twenty-five years of teaching speech to undergraduate students and business and professional people, I am convinced that the best way to learn the skill of speaking effectively is by preparing, practicing, and presenting speeches. For this reason I have intentionally written a text brief enough to allow the reader more time for involvement in the speechmaking process rather than in lengthy examination of theory.

Although *Speaking with a Purpose* presents up-to-date communication theory, it follows a step-by-step approach to preparing and delivering speeches. The text contains numerous examples excerpted from actual speeches chosen to represent a broad range of interests. As the title suggests, purpose and audience response are emphasized throughout the text.

The arrangement of the book is logical. Chapter 1 discusses the importance of speech, self-concept, the communication process, and listening. Chapters 2 through 8 follow a seven-step approach on how to prepare and deliver a speech. Chapter 9 deals with speaking to inform, and chapter 10 involves an in-depth study of persuasion and persuasive speaking.

A unique feature of chapter 11, the group communication chapter, is the inclusion of case problems as topics for discussion. These human-relations problems, which involve typical situations that discussants are likely to encounter in everyday life, have proven effective in stimulating group participation.

Speech and discussion evaluation forms, audience analysis guides, exercises, and specific speaking assignments are included at the ends of chapters.

I wish to thank the following for their valuable assistance in reviewing this book: Nancy Arnett, Brevard Community College; Alan C. Friedman, Belleville Area College; Gay Henry, State Technical Institute at Knoxville; Dan Mellinger, Cincinnati Technical College; Wendy Stocker, DeVry Institute of Technology; and Ronald H. Subeck, Wright College.

Arthur Koch

SPEAKING
WITH A
PURPOSE

chapter one

GETTING STARTED

In today's society, the person who can't communicate operates under a severe handicap. One of the main reasons employees lose their jobs is not that they lack the skill to do them but that they are unable to communicate effectively with their fellow workers. We constantly hear of the communication gap between government and citizens, between children and parents, between teachers and students, and between husbands and wives.

According to Dr. J. Ross Eshelman, chairman of the department of social psychology at Wayne State University, "Although there are a multitude of reasons given for divorce, such as adultery, drunkenness, sexual problems, and the like, in most cases these are problems caused by an inability of the marriage partners to communicate with each other."

What this all adds up to is obvious. If you want to get along better with others and if you want to be more successful in life, you will improve your chances considerably by learning to communicate more effectively. This book will deal primarily with speech communication, so the first thing to consider is how you learned to speak in the first place.

HOW SPEECH IS LEARNED

Because it is such an involved and complicated process there is no simple explanation as to exactly how speech is learned. However, most experts include both imitation and reinforcement as being of great importance in language development. You learned how to speak by imitating those around you. When you said or repeated words correctly, you were reinforced by words of praise, smiles, hugs, and other favorable responses. Your first reinforcers probably included your parents, brothers and sisters if you had any, and close relatives.

If you were typical, at about the age of one you first spoke single words, then two-word combinations, and later short phrases. By the time you were two, you had a vocabulary of from twenty-five to two hundred words. When you reached four, you spoke in full sentences, and by the time you entered the first grade, you had a vocabulary of about eight thousand words and communicated with four thousand of them. At some point during this period your speech habits and your attitude about self were influenced by others: friends of your parents, your own friends, babysitters, teachers, role models, and the like. If you were fortunate, the results were good speech habits and good self-concept.

This is not to say, however, that if you have a good self-concept you will not be nervous about giving a speech in front of others. Most people are concerned about whether they will do a good job in an important situation. Many professional speakers and entertainers experience some anxiety before they perform in public. However, they have learned to make use of that nervous energy to enhance their performances. The key here is to realize that some degree of nervousness is normal and that the more speeches you give, the more likely you will be to translate that nervous energy into delivering effective, purposeful speeches.

IMPROVING SELF-CONCEPT

As you can see, self-concept has a great deal to do with your ability to communicate. The better your self-concept, the more likely you will be to communicate positively and confidently. Following are specific suggestions for improving your self-concept.

1. Be willing to change. It is important that you view self-concept as a continuing process, as something that can be changed or reevaluated. The fact that you are enrolled in a course in speech indicates that you intend to improve your ability to communicate. If you do improve, it will have a positive effect on your self-concept.

2. Be willing to forgive yourself. All of us do "dumb" things at one time or another. To maintain a good self-concept, you must accept the fact that people make mistakes and try not to make the same mistake twice.

3. Set realistic goals. Don't expect too much of yourself. Remember, you're only human. Some people are constantly on a downer because they set goals for themselves that they cannot possibly achieve. You know what your limitations are. Don't be unrealistic and try to exceed them. And don't let others set unrealistic goals for you.

4. Develop your uniqueness. No matter how long the world continues there will never be another exactly like you. Therefore, strive only to be the very best "you" that you can. If you try to be someone else, the best you can hope for is second place.

5. Stand up for what you believe. Don't feel you always have to go along with the crowd. You don't necessarily have to get a pat on the back from society to be rewarded for what you do. You may feel better about yourself after supporting an unpopular cause.

6. View yourself in the proper perspective. Include both the real and ideal self in your self-concept. Ideally, your self-concept should be a clear perception of what you are now (real self) in relation to what you would like to be (ideal self). Although you might have a long way to go to reach your ultimate goal of what you want to become, if things are now going according to plan, you have reason to feel good about yourself.

THE COMMUNICATIVE ACT

There are five elements involved in the speech communication process: a speaker, a message, a channel (through which the message is sent), an audience, and a response. Each time a speaker communicates a message to others, these elements are present. In speaking situations these elements interact with each other. A simple speech situation can be summarized as follows:

1. A speaker wishes to communicate an idea.
2. The speaker encodes the idea in a message.
3. The message is sent through a channel to an audience.
4. The audience receives and decodes the message.
5. The audience responds to the message.

As you can see, the communication process is complex. In order to understand it better, it might be helpful to consider each of the five elements in the process separately.

Speaker

In the model above, the process of communication begins with a speaker who wishes to communicate an idea or some ideas. The image that the audience has of the speaker affects the message. Those in the audience who perceive a speaker as being a person of competence, integrity, and goodwill are most likely to believe what the speaker says.

Message

The second element in the communication process is the message. In order to insure that the listener attends to the message and understands it, the speaker must encode it in language that is both interesting and clear. Emphasis, variety, and descriptive language help make material interesting. Words that are specific and familiar help to make a message clear.

Channel

The channel is the means through which a message is transmitted. In the speaking situation the channel can involve all of the senses through which each member of the audience receives the information. Messages can be transmitted through hearing, seeing, smelling, tasting, and touching channels. A speaker can choose words that appeal to the audience's five senses, can include sensory aids in the message, or can add nonverbals to the message to make it more meaningful.

Audience

Without an audience, communication does not take place. A person stranded on an island can put a note in a bottle or stand on the shore screaming for help. However, unless someone reads the note or hears the screams, nothing will have been accomplished. This emphasizes the fact that all communication by a speaker must be audience centered. Unless a message is encoded with a specific audience in mind, it is liable to fail.

Response

In the final analysis, the success or failure of a communication is determined by audience response. The title of this book, *Speaking with a Purpose*, underlines the fact that in order to be successful when communicating, the speaker's purpose—to inform, to entertain, or to persuade—must be achieved. Therefore, the success or failure of a communication is measured by whether or not those in the audience are informed, entertained, or persuaded.

COMMUNICATION BREAKDOWNS

Communication breakdowns occur because of some failure in the communication process. If you invite a friend to your house for a Friday night fish fry and she comes Thursday night, the message you gave her was either inaccurate or misunderstood. If because you were daydreaming you fail to hear your instructor announce that the next class meeting has been called off, you might be the only class member present on that day. Communication breakdowns occur at some point during the speech situation. Perhaps the speaker has failed to analyze the audience correctly. Maybe the message has been encoded in technical terms that the audience cannot understand. Or it might be that the microphone the speaker is using significantly distorts the message. Any of these factors could result in a breakdown of communication.

Usually communication breakdowns can be traced to one of the five elements in the communication process: the speaker, message, channel, audience, or response. Consider the following situation and determine where the breakdown in communication occurred.

A businessman tells his secretary to have flowers sent to the grand opening of his friend's new branch office. The next day when he arrives at the grand opening, the businessman is shocked to find that the flowers he ordered are inscribed, ''Rest in Peace.'' He immediately drives to the florist to complain.

And the florist says, "You think that's bad? Somewhere in this city someone's lying in a coffin next to a floral arrangement labeled, "Good Luck in Your New Location!"

LISTENING

It is a frustrating thought that while you are delivering your speech, chances are that less than 15 percent of your audience will be actively listening to you. Most of them will be hearing you but not really listening. There is a considerable difference between hearing and listening. Hearing is the act of perceiving sounds, while listening involves making sense out of what you have heard.

Listening is an active process involving both concentration and thinking. Ineffective listening usually occurs because of a breakdown in one of these two areas. Either there is a barrier that interferes with the listener's concentration or the person has never learned to listen properly. Following are eight barriers to concentration in listening:

External Noise

External noise includes noises both inside and outside the listening area. Talking, footsteps, whispering, coughing, and street noise are some of the things that make it difficult to pay attention to a speaker. As a listener, you can avoid such distractions by arriving early enough at a speech or lecture to get a seat where you can see and hear easily. As a speaker, you can aid your audience by remaining silent until an emergency vehicle passes by or a bell stops ringing.

Internal Noise

Sometimes inner distractions caused by personal problems or concern about others can be so intense that it is extremely difficult to listen carefully. This internal noise can often be more distracting than a baby crying. When you are concerned about an upcoming test, a broken relationship, or a similar concern, you must redouble your efforts to concentrate.

Bias Toward Speaker

If a speaker's voice or appearance or mannerisms annoy you, listening carefully will become difficult. An instructor whose voice is raspy, who paces the floor, or who prefaces everything with "you know" can make a semester seem like an eternity. Work to overcome this listening barrier by concentrating on the content of the speech rather than the delivery.

Emotional Reaction

Sometimes a word or phrase can cause a negative response that can interfere with a listener's ability to concentrate. Loaded words like *honky* or *greaser* or the use of profanity can trigger emotional responses that interfere with a person's ability to listen effectively. Try to screen out emotional reactions by resolving to hear everything a speaker has to say before making a judgment.

Daydreaming

Who hasn't at one time or another drifted off into a pleasant daydream rather than paying attention? The tendency to daydream is influenced by two factors. First, a listener is able to think at a much faster rate than a speaker can speak. Consequently, while the speaker is talking at about 130 words per minute, the listener has plenty of thinking time left over. Second, attention is intermittent. That is, it stops and starts again at intervals. Daydreaming can be a serious barrier to listening. Learning to listen actively can help you avoid the tendency to daydream.

Faking Attention

Faking attention is a technique that is usually learned in the first or second grade. There students learn to sit at their desks while leaning forward with hands propped under their chins and an interested expression on their faces. Whether we learned it in school or not, we have all at one time or another been guilty of faking attention. The problem with faking attention is that it can be a difficult habit to break.

Fatigue

Listening is an active process, which requires the energy of the listener. If you are tired from too much studying or partying the night before, you will find it difficult to concentrate on what the speaker is saying. If you know that you will be attending an important speech or lecture, make sure that you are well rested.

Improper Note Taking

Taking notes ineffectively is worse than not taking notes at all. Students who attempt to write down too much of what a speaker is saying often wind up missing the point the speaker is trying to make. The way to avoid this problem is to develop note-taking skills.

WAYS TO IMPROVE LISTENING

Prepare to Listen

The first thing to do before attending a speech or lecture is to prepare yourself to listen. This means knowing something about the subject beforehand so that you can listen actively rather than passively. The first step in preparing to listen is to determine the subject from the title of the speech or lecture. Next you must think about what you already know about the subject. Chances are that you know something. If your knowledge is limited, you can go to the library or read your textbook to obtain information that will help you better understand what the speaker has to say. Preparing to listen is the first step to improving your listening skills. It is unlikely that you could listen with any degree of understanding to a subject you know "nothing" about.

Avoid Distractions

As indicated above, distractions can interfere with concentration and make it difficult to listen. To limit external distractions, arrive early enough to get a centrally located seat close to the speaker. If that is impossible, avoid sitting near windows or an entrance or exit.

Internal distractions are harder to screen out. The fact that you are aware that you are being bothered by them should alert you to redouble your efforts to concentrate.

Identify the Central Idea

If the speech or lecture you are listening to has been well prepared, the central idea should become immediately apparent. You might get a clue as to the central idea from the title or the purpose. However, whether the speaker states the central idea or it is implicit in the message, you as the listener must be aware of what it is. Ask yourself, "What is the point of this?" If you don't know, communication has not taken place.

Identify the Main Points

Most effective speeches involve a central idea supported by a number of main points. The listener's job is to sort out these main points from the supporting materials. This takes thinking and concentration. When identifying main points, listen for signals: "Some of the reasons that . . ." or "In addition . . ." Phrases like these tip you off to the fact that important ideas are forthcoming.

Think Along with the Speaker

In order to listen actively you must think along with the speaker. As you are listening, try to reconstruct the organizational pattern of the speech. Determine if the speaker is supporting each new idea with a variety of supporting materials. Relate what the speaker is saying to your own knowledge and interests. Responding to the speech in this way will not only improve your active listening but will provide insights that will aid you in developing your own speeches.

Take Effective Notes

Learning to take effective notes is an excellent way to improve your listening skills. Note taking promotes active listening and concentration. Rather than just listening passively to a speaker, the note taker must listen with the mind in order to identify the speaker's important ideas. It takes clear thinking and concentration to sort out main ideas from supporting details.

NOTE-TAKING TIPS

Write Down Only Important Ideas

A good speech is planned around a central idea and several main points. The central idea is usually stated in the introduction of the speech. Sometimes a speaker will also list the main points to be covered in the introduction. Listen for signals that indicate that main ideas are forthcoming. Words like *specifically*, *further*, and *first* indicate that a speaker is moving from one point to another.

Write Legibly

Sometimes note takers write so hurriedly that when they finish, they can't read their own notes. If your notes are illegible, you are probably writing down too much.

Keep Up

If you find that you are falling behind in your note taking, skip a few lines and begin again. Later, when you expand your notes, you can fill in the missing information.

Use Your Own Words

One of the best ways to show that you understand something is to be able to explain it in your own words. When you translate the ideas of another into your own vocabulary, they will be easier to understand and remember.

Be Brief

A common mistake among inexperienced note takers is the tendency to write down too much. Don't try to write down everything the speaker says. A set of notes should be a summary of a speaker's main ideas.

Don't Erase

Rather than wasting time erasing, draw a line through the mistake and continue. Remember, the notes you are taking are for your own use. If you want your notes to be neat, you can rewrite or type them later.

Don't Worry about Spelling

If you're not sure about how a word is spelled, write it phonetically. You can check the spelling later when you expand your notes.

Date Your Notes

Whether you are taking notes on a lecture or a public speech, you should get into the habit of dating them. This will enable you to pinpoint a missed lecture or the specific date of a speech.

Expand Your Notes

If the notes you are taking are for the purpose of helping you remember information or to aid you in studying for an exam, it is wise to expand them as soon after a lecture as possible.

EXERCISES

1. Relate a personal experience that helped you to perceive a positive image of yourself. The story you tell can be true, partly true, or fictitious. The important thing is that your audience should be able to perceive your reaction to the situation and understand how that reaction gave you a clear picture of yourself.

2. Relate a personal experience that caused you to perceive a negative image of yourself. Follow the suggestions above.

3. Tell about someone you know or once knew who said something to you that made you feel positive about yourself.

4. Tell about someone who said something to you that made you feel negative about yourself.

5. Tell about a time when you said something to someone that boosted his or her self-esteem. Explain what made you aware of the effect of your statement. Indicate whether you made the statement intentionally.

6. Tell about a time when you said something that lowered a person's self-esteem. Explain what made you aware of the effect of your statement. Indicate whether you made the statement intentionally.

7. Cite two examples of communication breakdowns. Indicate the causes of the breakdowns. Explain what could have been done to improve the communication in each case.

8. Tell of an instance when a barrier to listening kept you from concentrating at a speech or lecture. Did you try to overcome the barrier? What did you do?

chapter two

DETERMINE YOUR PURPOSE AND SUBJECT

In order to develop an effective speech you must have a clear purpose in mind. The title of this book, *Speaking with a Purpose*, emphasizes the importance of purpose in oral communication. Your aim as a speaker should be to fulfill a purpose by achieving a desired response. Your success in informing, entertaining, or persuading must always be measured in terms of the response your receiver gives to your message. Beginning speakers often fail because they pay too little attention to purpose and audience response when planning their speeches. Following are the major purposes in speaking:

1. To entertain—to elicit a pleasurable response, to provoke curiosity, to provide suspense, or to amuse. Treating a serious subject lightly or a light subject seriously and describing an unusual or exciting experience are examples of communication to entertain.

2. To inform—to add to the knowledge or understanding of the listener. Demonstrating how to do something, explaining a process, reporting on a meeting, and describing an event are examples of communication to inform.

3. To persuade—To convince, to reinforce, or to actuate. Since persuasion is more complex than entertainment or information, the three types of persuasion will be treated separately.

   a. To convince—to change your listener's opinions or to commit them to a point of view about which they are undecided. Persuasion to convince occurs frequently in debate and in problem-solving discussion. In both, information is given to listeners in an attempt to get them to change their minds or to form an opinion on something about which they are undecided. Persuasion to convince relies heavily on a logical approach using reasoning, statistics, testimony, comparison, and factual examples.

   b. To reinforce—to arouse and invigorate an audience already in agreement with the speaker's point of view. A speech at a pep rally in the school auditorium before a football or basketball game is a good example of persuasion to reinforce. The students do not have to be convinced about the importance of their team's winning. The idea is to strengthen their attitude about winning, to build a fire under them so that they are prepared emotionally and enthusiastically for the game. Persuasion to reinforce largely employs a psychological approach—appealing to the attitudes, beliefs, sentiments, and motives of the audience.

   c. To actuate—to put into action. In the previous example the speaker's job is to stimulate the members of the student audience to become even more excited than they already are about the upcoming game. However, they are not given specific instructions as to what to do in terms of that excitement. In persuasion to actuate the audience should be told exactly what action you want accomplished. A speech by the coach to the team in the locker room before the game is a good example of persuasion to actuate. The team is told specifically to go out and "win one for the alma mater." The speech to actuate asks the audience, to buy, to sell, to join, to march, or the like. While it can employ persuasion to convince or to reinforce or both, it is by far more successful when directed to an audience who already agree. Obviously, if you want to get your audience to do something, you are bound to be more successful if they are already predisposed to act that way.

SELECTING A SUBJECT

Once you clearly understand the general purpose of your speech, you are ready to choose a subject. There will undoubtedly be times when you will be asked to deliver a speech on a topic that has already been determined. For example, you are asked to give a report on a convention you attended as a delegate. Or as a member of a symposium you are assigned to speak on one aspect of a subject. In a different situation the occasion might determine what your subject will be. However, more often than not, you will need to select your own subject. When doing so, your decision should be based on a number of considerations:

1. Is the subject suited to my purpose?
2. Is the subject interesting to me?
3. Am I qualified to speak on this subject?
4. Will my audience find this subject interesting?
5. Will my audience find this subject useful?
6. Is my subject sufficiently restricted?

Is the Subject Suited to my Purpose?

Suppose you are asked to deliver a speech whose general purpose is to inform. Because you know how to fillet fish and have access to some that have been freshly caught, you decide to show your audience how to fillet. Since your purpose is to inform, the result should be that everyone in the audience will know how to fillet a fish when you are done with your speech. That, of course, is highly unlikely. Filleting a fish is one of those skills you must learn by doing. You would have to show them how to fillet and then guide them as they practiced on fish of their own. Besides the problem of getting a fish and knife for everyone in your audience, the whole procedure would be messy and possibly dangerous. A demonstration on filleting would be better suited as a speech to persuade, where you could show how easy it is and therefore stimulate an interest on the part of your audience to learn more about it. Or you might deliver a speech to entertain by demonstrating how to fillet while humorously botching the job.

Is My Subject Interesting to Me?

Whenever possible choose a subject you find interesting. Enthusiasm is a key factor to successful speaking. If you talk enthusiastically about something, this enthusiasm is bound to rub off on your audience. Are you excited about a particular kind of music or art form? Are you into break dancing or disco? Do you jog or weightlift? Collect coins? With a little imagination and some effort you can make what interests you interesting for your audience.

When you have difficulty finding a subject that interests you, try a technique called brainstorming. Take out a blank sheet of paper and jot down as many potential speech topics as you can. Don't worry about the quality of these topics; aim for quantity. After you have listed as many as you can, put the sheet away for at least eight hours. When you return to it, you may very well find that you have listed a number of topics of interest to you that you hadn't thought about.

Am I Qualified to Speak on this Subject?

The fact that you are interested in a subject does not necessarily mean that you are qualified to speak on it. If your interest is recent, you might lack sufficient knowledge or experience to prepare the subject effectively. In some cases it might be better to select a subject with which you are more familiar. Did you grow up on a farm? Were you born in a different country? Do you have special skills in real estate, music, computer, or sewing? Were you in the armed forces? Sometimes the perfect speech topic is so close that the speaker doesn't see it.

Will My Audience Find This Subject Interesting?

It takes little effort to pay attention to a subject that is interesting. Therefore you will hold the attention of your audience if your subject is interesting to them. If you are not sure it will be, you must work to make it so. An effective way to do this is to use attention factors—humor, novelty, suspense, and the like. You will find a discussion of attention factors on pages 60–63.

Will My Audience Find This Subject Useful?

People will willingly pay attention to a communication if they expect to gain something useful from doing so. Consider your own experience. Have you ever followed a set of instructions on how to operate a computer, bake a cake, or ferment your own wine? Have you ever attended a lecture on what to expect on the final exam? Have you ever bought a do-it-yourself book and tried to follow the "simplified instructions"? Did you pay attention? Of course you did. If the subject you choose will benefit your audience in some way, it will quite likely hold their attention. If you feel that the usefulness of your subject will not be readily apparent to your audience, tell them in your introduction how they will benefit from listening to your speech.

Is My Subject Sufficiently Restricted?

In most cases you will be given a definite time limit when you are asked to give a speech. If you exceed this time limit appreciably you are bound to annoy your audience. Many beginning speakers try to cover too much in the time available to them. It is far better to deal with a restricted subject in detail than to cover too many points. Remember, if you cover too much material without supporting it adequately, your audience is unlikely to remember it no matter how long your speech is.

SPECIFIC PURPOSE

After you have chosen your subject in accordance with the considerations above, you are ready to formulate a specific purpose. Earlier I classified the general purposes for speaking: to entertain, to inform, and to persuade. Specific purposes tell more precisely what your intent is. They indicate in more detail exactly what you hope to accomplish. Note the following examples:

1. General purpose: to entertain
    Specific purposes:
    a. to amuse my audience by explaining how to wash a bull elephant
    b. to hold my audience in suspense while telling of the time I was robbed
    c.   to amaze my audience with a demonstration of magic
    d. to fascinate my audience with a story about my first parachute jump

2. General purpose: to inform

   Specific purposes:

   a. to explain the art of tree dwarfing
   b. to demonstrate how to make an omelet
   c. to show how to take an effective snapshot
   d. to report the results of a recent experiment

3. General purpose: to persuade

   Specific purposes:

   a. to motivate my audience to contribute to CARE
   b. to prove to my audience that my new plan for ending the arms race will work
   c. to increase my audience's reverence for our flag
   d. to modify my audience's attitude about socialized medicine

Note that the specific purposes above are phrases that begin with the infinitive form of a verb which clearly relates to one of the three general purposes of speech. Thus, speeches to entertain, amuse, fascinate, amaze, delight; speeches to inform explain, make clear, demonstrate, report; and speeches to persuade motivate, prove, increase, modify; and so on.

THE CENTRAL IDEA

Once you have phrased your specific-purpose statement, it is wise to state the central idea of your speech in a complete sentence. The central idea may be thought of as the thesis, the key statement, or the controlling idea of the speech. Since it is related to the specific purpose of your speech, at times the two may be similar.

Stating the central idea as a complete sentence will help you plan your communication more effectively. Following are three central-idea statements related to three of the specific-purpose statements above.

Specific purpose—to amuse my audience by telling them how to wash a bull elephant.

Central idea—washing a bull elephant isn't all that easy.

Specific purpose—to explain the art of tree dwarfing.

Central idea—the secret of tree dwarfing is twofold: cutting the root and branch system properly and maintaining the tree correctly.

Specific purpose: to motivate my audience to contribute to CARE.

Central idea: CARE is the most efficient and effective charity in the world.

As you can see, the central-idea statement is a clear statement of the way in which you plan to develop your speech. For example, the first purpose above is to entertain, specifically to amuse the audience by telling them how to wash a bull elephant. The central idea—washing a bull elephant isn't all that easy—implies that the speech will involve some of the humorous problems that could arise when trying to wash the elephant. The second purpose—to explain the art of tree drawfing—is to inform. Its central idea indicates that the speech will deal with the two most important principles in tree dwarfing: cutting the roots and branches properly and maintaining the tree correctly. The third specific purpose—to motivate my audience to contribute to CARE—is to actuate. The central idea clearly indicates that you will develop the speech by talking about the efficiency and effectiveness of CARE.

EXERCISES

State whether the primary purpose in each of the following situations is (a) to inform, (b) to entertain, (c) to convince, (d) to reinforce, or (e) to actuate. Be prepared to explain and defend your answer.

1. The reading of a will
2. A TV shampoo commercial
3. A newscast
4. A debate
5. A eulogy at a funeral
6. An ornithology lecture
7. A TV soap opera
8. A campaign speech

Write a central-idea statement and specific-purpose statement for any of the following subjects as your instructor directs.

1. Alcoholism
2. Study habits
3. Crime
4. Listening
5. Education
6. Hobbies

chapter three

AUDIENCE ANALYSIS

After you have selected a subject and determined your purpose, you are ready to think of the speech in terms of your audience. An audience is an indispensable part of communication. If your audience fails to understand or pay attention to your message, communication does not take place. Therefore, when you develop your speech, do so with your audience in mind.

A speech that is prepared with a specific audience in mind is one that is audience-centered. To aid in preparing an audience-centered speech, ask yourself the questions discussed in this chapter.

WHO EXACTLY IS MY AUDIENCE?

As you prepare the content of your speech, consider who is in your audience. Your boss or teacher? Your coworkers or classmates? Yourself? Even if there is only one male or one female in an otherwise all-female or all-male audience, you must consider this person when preparing your speech. A surprising number of communications fail because the sender has been unclear as to the composition of his or her audience.

Take the case of George Scott, assistant cashier of a small midwestern bank. George came home in a state of dejection one night after having been passed over for promotion for the third time. He called his sister-in-law Phyllis, a close friend of the bank president's wife, and asked her to try to find out why. She learned the following:

George considered himself a great story teller and was particularly fond of ethnic jokes. He often told these jokes, both at the office and at holiday and other office get-togethers. What George failed to realize was that a number of people, including the bank president, found this sort of humor at the expense of others patently offensive. Whenever an opportunity for advancement occurred, George was rejected as being too insensitive. He paid a high price for not knowing his audience.

Consider your audience carefully, make note of their interests, consider their backgrounds, knowledge, and attitudes toward your subject and then develop your speech accordingly.

WHAT RESPONSE CAN I REASONABLY EXPECT
FROM MY AUDIENCE?

No matter how good a speech looks on paper or how well it is delivered, its success or failure must always be measured in terms of audience response. A salesperson who doesn't sell the product will soon be out of a job, the comedienne who doesn't evoke laughter will fall flat on her face, and the politician who doesn't get votes will not get elected. Therefore, when developing your speech, you must always consider your purpose in terms of audience response.

Some responses might be unattainable. Your audience might not have the background or experience necessary for you to be able to teach them how to repair a computer or sew a dress. A lack of time or resources might prevent you from showing your audience how to give a permanent or tile a floor. Your audience's attitude might be so opposed to your subject that they reject it at the outset. An example of the last would be trying to promote the legalization of marijuana in the United States. While some in your audience would be for it, others would be impossible to approach. In such cases you would be better off choosing another, more realistic purpose that could achieve a reasonable response.

WILL MY AUDIENCE FIND THIS SUBJECT USEFUL?

People willingly pay attention if they will gain something from doing so. You pay attention to the directions for filling out your income tax because you have something to gain if you do—and something to lose if you don't. You listen to a dull story told by your boss or prospective in-law and laugh because it is in your best interest to do so.

If for some reason members of your audience *need* to know the information you will be giving them in your speech, tell them they do. If they will prevent possible costly repair to their cars by engaging in a do-it-yourself lubricating program, if they have a responsibility to act against the growing problem of child abuse, or if they might possibly save a life by taking a Red Cross CPR course, let them know at the beginning of the speech. To show an audience how to react to an accident in the home and then explain to them only at the conclusion of your speech that the majority of accidents occur in the home would be to leave a number of those in your audience thinking, ''I guess I should have listened.''

Whenever possible, give your listener a reason for listening, and do it during the introduction to your speech.

WILL MY AUDIENCE FIND THIS SUBJECT INTERESTING?

The second reason that people pay attention is to satisfy an interest. Less effort is required to pay attention to what is interesting than to what is useful. Consider your own experience. Have you ever watched an unimaginative educational film because you knew there would be an exam about it? Have you listened to an uninteresting lecture because you knew it would have an effect on your grade? How much did you learn in that course? How much do you remember? In both cases you had, in effect, something to gain in paying attention. Did it pay off? Now compare the uninteresting educational film or the lecture to the educational TV program, "Sesame Street." It is estimated that "Sesame Street" has a viewing audience of ten million. The people who write and produce the program handle their material in such an interesting way that paying attention (and thus learning) is no longer a chore—it is fun. Your job as a speaker is to develop your material interestingly. While you can do this with someone you know quite well, how can you do it with strangers?

If you are familiar with the subject you have chosen, you should be able to make an educated guess.

Suppose you choose to speak about one of your two hobbies, raising tropical fish or restoring antique cars. The majority of your friends have shown more interest in your antique cars than in your fish. Some might have even changed the subject when you asked if they wanted to see your baby swordtails. Certainly, a general audience would have greater initial interest in antique cars.

This, however, does not mean you could not choose to speak about raising tropical fish. You can do it effectively if you build your audience's interest to gain and maintain their attention. You might begin by introducing your listeners to the piranha, one of the most interesting fish you own. A description of this voracious, sometimes maneating creature as even more dangerous than the great white shark is a surefire attention getter.

WHAT IS MY AUDIENCE'S KNOWLEDGE OF MY SUBJECT?

Considering what your listeners already know about your subject is an important part of audience analysis. A too technical approach could leave them thoroughly confused; repeating what they already know is sure to bore them.

If your audience has little or no knowledge of your subject, you must explain unfamiliar terminology and concepts to them. Keep in mind that this lack of knowledge will have an effect on their ability to respond. You could not expect those in your audience who have little idea of what is under the hood of a car to learn how to adjust a set of points or time a car after your speech to demonstrate. Nor could the nonsewer be expected to know how to install a zipper or cuff a pair of pants after a speech to demonstrate. Your educated guess as to the audience's knowledge of your subject should be an important consideration in terms of your choice of subject and purpose for each speech you make.

WHAT DEMOGRAPHIC CHARACTERISTICS SHOULD I CONSIDER ABOUT MY AUDIENCE?

The word *demography* is derived from the Greek word *demos*, meaning "people." The demographic consideration of your audience has to do with their vital statistics: age, education, beliefs, special interests, and so on. These characteristics can often help you in determining how to handle your subject. For example, as a rule, young people tend to be more physically active than older people, more inclined to engage in sports rather than watch them. Consequently, when talking about a particular sport, you might treat it as a participation sport for a younger audience and as a spectator sport for an older group.

The educational level of your audience could be important to you for a number of reasons. One of these has to do with the relationship between education and vocabulary. You must speak to an audience in familiar words that they can instantly understand. For example, you wouldn't explain the process of osmosis to your eleven-year-old sister in the same way you'd explain it to your college speech class. Another consideration is that a well-educated audience will be more aware of vital issues and current events than a less educated one will.

Do those in your audience have similar attitudes and beliefs? Do they have special interests in common? Are they rich or poor, Democrat or Republican, conservative or liberal? Any of these demographic characteristics might be important to you as you prepare your speech. Remember, the success of your speech is always determined in terms of audience response. Did your audience get the information you wanted them to have? Were they entertained? Did you get them to take the action you wanted? The more you know about your audience, the more likely it will be that you will achieve your purpose.

IS MY AUDIENCE'S ATTITUDE FAVORABLE, INDIFFERENT, OR OPPOSED?

A Favorable Audience

Perhaps the greatest advantage to dealing with a favorable audience is that they are usually both supportive and attentive. Your goal when communicating to them is to reinforce their positive attitudes. If they enjoy humor, the more effectively you entertain them with your humor, the more successful you will be. If they would benefit from some tips on simple car maintenance, their satisfaction will be measured by how clearly you can explain your directions. The more effectively you can reinforce their positive attitudes, the more likely you will be to move them to action.

An Indifferent Audience

When an audience is indifferent, your job is to stimulate their interest. This can best be done by explaining the usefulness of the subject to them, by gaining their attention with a fresh imaginative approach, or by a combination of both. Take this action as soon as possible in your introduction. The sooner you can get the audience on your side, the better.

A successful speech to an indifferent audience was given by Erik Jackson, a second-year photography student. From conversations he had with them, Erik was aware that many of his classmates did not share his interest in photography and did not own expensive cameras or equipment. So, rather than delivering a complicated speech involving f-stop or light meters, Erik decided to give his speech class information about photography that would be useful to them no matter what kind of equipment they had.

Erik began his speech by showing those in his audience several pages of pictures from a photo album. He had enlarged each of the pictures so that they could easily be seen, even by those in the back of the room. He called his classmates' attention to the fact that other than there being different people in each, the photos were very much alike. In each snapshot people stood rigidly together in a line with smiles on their faces.

Next Erik showed the class a few variations of the first pictures he had shown. Although the people in them were the same, these snapshots were much more interesting than the first set. In some the arrangement of people was much more interesting. In others the background made the group stand out much more vividly. By explaining about camera angle, posing, and picture balance, Erik demonstrated to his audience that with a little imagination they could take pictures that were more interesting.

An Opposed Audience

The hardest audience to deal with is one that includes many who disagree with your point of view or your subject. If you find that this is the case and you have a choice in the matter, you might consider choosing another topic. If you have no alternative, however, or are enthusiastic about your subject, concentrate on presenting your material so that you provide information that will make your audience less opposed toward your subject than they were when you started. Be aware that there is little change in viewpoint among those who listen to things with which they strongly disagree. Two useful suggestions for dealing with audiences opposed to a topic are (1) to establish a common ground with your audience and (2) to provide them with information that will help to clear up any lack of understanding or misinformation they might have. Consider the following example:

Betty White, a college sophomore, decided to deliver a speech on one of her favorite subjects, opera. In talking to her classmates, she found that many in her audience were "turned off" by her topic. One student named Jeff even told her that he intended to cut class on the day of her speech because opera, especially Wagnerian opera, Betty's favorite, made him sick.

On the day of her speech Betty identified with many in her audience by beginning:

"Four years ago I never would have dreamed of delivering a speech about opera to anyone. But then I found out an interesting fact. I didn't like opera because I did not know anything about it. Since then, the more I learn about opera the more I like it. And my guess is that when you get to know enough about it, you'll like it too."

Betty realized that if she was going to reach those in her audience who were opposed to her subject, she would have to identify with them and turn them on to the good things about opera with a fresh, imaginative approach. She prepared carefully and thoughtfully and delivered a humorous plot summary of Wagner's opera *Tannhauser*, which ended, to even Jeff's delight, with the heroine's getting stabbed right between the two big trees.

Betty took what many in her audience thought would be a boring topic and made it exciting and interesting. She used humor, novelty, conflict, and suspense to hold their attention. The result was a successful speech.

In order to communicate successfully to an audience you must first understand them. Put yourself in their shoes. If you do, you will be much more likely to achieve your purpose. If you don't, you are liable to end up speaking to yourself and only a few others.

EXERCISES

1. Analyze five different magazines to determine the kinds of audiences to which they appeal.

2. Prepare a list of topics that would be interesting to your audience.

3. Prepare a list of topics that would be useful to your audience.

4. Analyze your class as an audience. In what ways are they similar? In what ways do they differ?

5. Pick a highly controversial issue such as abortion. Write a statement that favors or opposes it. Estimate how many in your class would agree with your statement, be indifferent to it, or oppose it. Survey the class to check your answer.

6. Analyze a popular TV show. To what age group is it directed? To what intelligence level would it appeal? Describe the characteristics of a "typical" viewer.

AUDIENCE ANALYSIS FORM

Name_____ Date_____

Title of Speech _____

(Answer each question completely)

THE COMMUNICATOR

1. Why have I chosen this subject?

2. What qualifies me to deal with this subject?

THE MESSAGE

3. What is my specific purpose?

4. What response can I reasonably expect?

THE AUDIENCE

5. Who is my audience?

6. Will my audience find this subject interesting?

7. Will my audience find this subject useful?

8. What is the **audience**'s probable knowledge of my subject?

9. What characteristics of my audience should I consider in preparing my subject?

10. Is my audience's attitude toward this subject favorable, indifferent, or opposed?

Figure 3-1 Audience analysis form.

AUDIENCE ANALYSIS EVALUATION FORM

Name_____

1. What was the communicator's subject?

2. How interesting was this subject to you?

    |___|___|___|___|___|
    low   high

3. How useful was this subject to you?

    |___|___|___|___|___|
    low   high

4. How effectively did the communicator get attention during introduction?

    |___|___|___|___|___|
    low   high

5. How much preparation was put into this communication?

    |___|___|___|___|___|
    low   high

6. What was the communicator's specific purpose? (One simple, declarative sentence)

7. How effective was the conclusion to the communication?

    |___|___|___|___|___|
    low   high

8. How well did the communicator accomplish his purpose?

    |___|___|___|___|___|
    low   high

COMMENTS:

Figure 3-2   Audience analysis evaluation form.

The audience analysis form and the audience analysis evaluation form shown in Figures 3-1 and 3-2 are designed to aid you in better understanding your audience. Fill out a copy of the audience analysis form during the planning of your speech. Many of the answers you put down on the form will be educated guesses about your audience.

Have your classmates fill out the audience analysis evaluation form to give you feedback as to how successful you were in analyzing and adapting to your audience.

chapter four

SUPPORTING YOUR IDEAS

One of the best ways to improve your effectiveness as a speaker is to learn how to select and use supporting materials. Supporting materials are necessary to make your ideas clear or persuasive to your literature. Although there are different lists of supporting materials, most experts in the speech field agree on these six: examples, explanation, statistics, testimony, comparison/contrast, and visual aids. You have most likely used each of these during your lifetime, perhaps without being aware that there was a specific name for each. Suppose, for example, that you want to convince your parents that your new boyfriend is the ideal male. You might use any of the six supporting devices to support your assertion:

Example: "Mom and Dad, you're going to love Chris. He's one of the kindest people I've ever met. He puts in eight hours of volunteer work a week at the Mayville Nursing Home, he's a big brother to an eleven-year-old boy from the inner city, and he supports a little Cambodian child through the Christian Children's Fund."

Explanation: "I see Chris as the perfect male. The consideration with which he treats me makes me feel special and loved, and his sensitivity to music, art, literature, and nature make him a fascinating person to be with."

Statistics: "Chris is 6 feet tall, he weighs 180 pounds, and he makes over thirty thousand dollars a year."

Testimony: "Rabbi Silberg, who is on the board of directors of Mayville Nursing Home, says Chris is one of the hardest working and best liked volunteers they have."

Comparison/Contrast: "Chris isn't like any man I've ever met. The others have been interested in doing only what they want and in satisfying their own egos. Chris believes that love is a sharing, and that's the way he acts."

Visual Aids: "Here are some snapshots of Chris. Doesn't he have a pleasant, open face? And, did you notice how neatly he dresses?"

EXAMPLES

When wisely chosen, the example is without a doubt the most effective and versatile of all the supporting devices. You would be wise to use at least one example as a support for every main point in your speech. An example is actually a typical sample selected to show the nature or character of the rest. Examples can be brief or detailed, factual or hypothetical, and humorous or serious. If an example is factual and familiar to your audience, you need only to cite it briefly since they know the details. If the example is hypothetical or unfamiliar to your audience, you must develop it in enough detail so that the point your story makes is clear to them. For instance, if you are talking about the problem of child abuse, and a highly publicized case has recently occurred in your community, you need only to mention the case briefly but clearly. If, however, the instance of abuse occurred in a different location or a number of years earlier, you might have to tell it as a short story with facts, names, and dates. Detailed examples are often called illustrations. These illustrations or stories can take the form of anecdotes, personal experiences, allegories, or parables. Using illustrations in your speech can provide your audience with clear mental pictures of particular instances or events.

When selecting supporting materials for your speech, look for appropriate and interesting examples that are clear, concise, and to the point. Note how the following examples support the speaker's central idea: Every adult American should have an up-to-date will.

Brief Factual Example

Although a will can be made out by an individual or for as little as twenty-five dollars by a lawyer, over 50 percent of all Americans die without ever having made one. No doubt, many of them planned to but just put it off. For example, Supreme Court Justice Fred Vinson died without a will, and Senator Robert Kerr was in the process of writing one when he died unexpectedly.

Brief Hypothetical Example

There are many reasons for keeping your will up to date. Suppose that you name your sister as executor, and she dies, moves away, or is too ill to serve? What if federal or state laws or court interpretations of them change? Suppose you move to a state where inheritance tax laws differ? All these are reasons for reviewing your will whenever major changes occur.

Detailed Factual Example

Uncle George died about a year ago. He had never made a will, and this created some real problems for his wife, Aunt Edna, and their three minor children. The checking and savings accounts were in my uncle's name and the bank wouldn't let Aunt Edna draw out any money. Because the deed for their house listed them as "tenants in common," the children were due to inherit two-thirds of the house. The result of this was that nobody would lend Aunt Edna money for a second mortgage on the house, and she couldn't sell it because as minors, the children couldn't "sign off" ownership in favor of their mother. The whole matter had to be taken to probate court, where it still is. To date, Aunt Edna has yet to see a single penny of Uncle George's estate and has borrowed over ten thousand dollars from her relatives.

Detailed Hypothetical Example

John Jones, a widower with four children, remarries. He registers everything he owns in joint ownership with the new Mrs. Jones knowing that she will provide for the children if he dies. A year later both are killed in an auto accident. To compound the tragedy, Mrs. Jones survives her husband by one hour, and his assets revert to her as co-owner. Unfortunately, Mrs. Jones had not made out a will, and the entire estate goes by law to her only blood relative, a cousin she doesn't even like. Because there was no will none of Mr. Smith's assets went to his children, since Mrs. Smith was related to them only as a stepmother.

EXPLANATION

The purpose of explanation is to make an idea clear or understandable. Obviously then, explanation qualifies as an excellent supporting device. Explanation can involve a number of different forms. It can include exposition, analysis, definition, and description.

Exposition

Exposition may be defined as communication which gives information to your listeners in order to increase their knowledge or their understanding of a situation or process. A speech on how to use a fly rod, bake a cake, lower a ceiling, or make a fortune in the stock market will in each case employ exposition. When a gas station attendant gives you directions on how to get to a nearby city, and you in turn pass his explanation on to the driver of the car you are traveling in, both conversations have largely involved exposition.

Analysis

Analysis is the process of explaining something by breaking it down into its parts and examining them. You use analysis when you explain how something works. If, for example, you want to convince your listeners to install inexpensive, homemade burglar alarm systems in their cars, you would have to give them a clear idea of what is involved in this system and how it would work. Another form of evaluation with which you are all familiar is the critique, or review. Perhaps you have attended a movie, play, or concert and afterwards totally disagreed with the review it received. Keep this in mind when you are using analysis as a supporting device so that you might do so as objectively as possible.

Definition

When you use a term or concept that is unfamiliar to your audience, you must define it either in your own words or in the words of someone else. Be careful not to use words in your definition that are more difficult to understand than the term or concept you are defining. For the sake of imaginativeness and interest, avoid using dictionary definitions. They are often overly formal and complex. Keep your definitions clear and to the point using wording that your listeners can readily understand.

Description

Description makes use of the five sensory appeals (the five senses being taste, hearing, sight, touch, and smell) to make clear to your listener exactly what is being communicated. Although it isn't necessary to appeal to all five in each communication, the more of them to which you appeal, the more effective the communication. Effective description can create images or word pictures in the minds of your listeners.

STATISTICS

When used correctly, statistics can be an effective means of support. However, unless your statistics are both valid and reliable, they should not be used.

It was Benjamin Disraeli who said, "There are three kinds of lies: lies, damned lies, and statistics." His comment points up the fact that statistics can often be manipulated to support almost any assertion. For this reason it is wise to document the statistics you are using. This means indicating when and by whom the statistics were compiled. It is quite likely that there are those in your audience who have in the past been deceived by statistics. Put them at ease by using statistics that are up to date and compiled by a reputable source.

This, however, does not mean that you must document every statistic that you use. Some statistics are so widely accepted that few would question them. For instance, if you told your audience that over 60 percent of those killed in automobile accidents in the United States during 1985 had some alcohol in their blood, or that a divorce rate in 1985 of over 45 percent makes marriage a bad risk, it would be unlikely that anyone in your audience would find either figure too high. It is up to you to decide when or when not to document your statistics. Try to make the statistics you use as interesting and uncomplicated as possible. Remember, it is your job as the speaker to maintain your listener's attention. Here are some suggestions to follow when using statistics.

Dramatize Your Statistics

If you can present your statistics in a dramatic or vivid way, they are more likely to be understood and remembered by your audience. When stated unimaginatively, statistics can often be quite dry. When stated in terms that a listener can visualize, they can be quite thought provoking. Consider this example from a student speech called "The Danger from Toxics."

According to 1984 Environmental Protection Agency estimates, there are 6000 active and 30,000 abandoned hazardous waste sites in the United States and over 70,000 underground gasoline tanks that are leaking. Over one-third of all U.S. groundwater has been contaminated by 200,000 wasteponds and landfills and 200 million septic systems. And over 500,000 rural households have drinking water so contaminated that it would be declared unsafe for swimming at a public beach.

According to a 1982 OSHA Management Information System report, OSHA, the Occupational Safety and Health branch of the Environmental Protection Agency lessened safety in the work place by easing standards designed to protect the health of workers. For example, in June 1983 standards on cotton dust were lowered, making an additional 362,100 workers vulnerable to "brown lung," a crippling and sometimes fatal lung disease caused by inhalation of cotton dust. Furthermore, OSHA has declined to regulate ethylene oxide, a chemical that exposes 150,000 workers daily to increased risks of leukemia, lymphoma, and genetic damage.

Statistics presented in this manner are dramatic, easier to visualize, and therefore more likely to be remembered. To maintain credibility when presenting statistics as shocking as these, indicate the source of your information.

Round Off Your Statistics

Remember, unless you repeat your statistics, your listeners will hear them only once. For this reason it is a good idea to round off complex numbers. Although it may be more exacting, instead of saying that the medium income of police officers in this city is $25,167, round if off to "around $25,200" or "slightly over $25,000." In the following excerpt the student-speaker rounds off the statistics she uses to support her proposition that the rich have gotten richer under the Reagan administration's tax bill.

A recent study by the joint committee on taxation has indicated that the Reagan tax bill will have cost the Treasury $750 billion by the end of fiscal year 1986. The large majority of the benefits will go to the richest Americans.

Table 4-1   Crime—A Look At The Odds

YOUR CHANCE OF BEING MURDERED:

This year	1 in 10,000
In a lifetime	1 in 133
If you're a black male	1 in 21
If you're a white female	1 in 369

YOUR CHANCE OF BEING ASSAULTED, RAPED, OR ROBBED

This year	1 in 31
If you make less than $3000	1 in 18
If you make more than $25,000	1 in 37
If you're black	1 in 25
If you're between 16 and 19	1 in 15

Source: Justice Department 1985 Report

The wealthiest 6 percent of taxpayers will receive over 35 percent of the benefits while the bottom 40 percent will get only 8 percent. In fact, families making $22,000 per year or less will actually be paying higher taxes owing to the regressive social security tax.

Display Your Statistics Visually

Statistical data that are complex should be presented on charts, tables, graphs, or diagrams in order to help your audience grasp what is being presented. A student used the table reproduced here (Table 4-1) (in a much larger form) to show more clearly the increasing risk we all face as potential victims of violent crime.

TESTIMONY

We live in a complex age, an age of specialization. For this reason it is often wise for nonexpert speakers to support their ideas with the testimony of others who are expert. The testimony of an expert or authority on a particular subject carries the weight of that person's education and experience. Few of us would quarrel with an opthalmologist who recommended that we switch to bifocals or an auto mechanic who told us that we needed a new vacuum advance. Unless we questioned their honesty or competency, we would have no reason to doubt their judgment. Consequently, when you are delivering a speech, support your opinions if need be with the opinions of others more expert than you to add credibility to your presentation.

When supporting your point of view with the testimony of others, you can either quote them verbatim or paraphrase what they have said in your own words. The decision is up to you. There are, however, two instances when it is better to quote directly than to paraphrase: (1) when the person you are quoting has said it so well you cannot possibly say it better, and (2) when the testimony is controversial, and you want your audience to hear it straight from the source. Otherwise, it is perfectly acceptable to state the testimony in your own words. When doing so, be careful to paraphrase the testimony of another both fairly and accurately. As a speaker, you have a responsibility to be honest and straightforward.

If the experts you are citing are likely to be unfamiliar to those in your audience, give facts about them that will establish their credibility. Your listeners will give more heed to what Dr. Carl J. George, chairman of the department of psychology at the University of Wisconsin and author of *Knowing Your Child*, has to say about teenage suicide than they will to what Carl J. George or even Dr. Carl J. George has to say.

Although it is often important that the authority you are citing is up to date, this is not always necessary. It can often be very effective to back up your point of view by citing an authority from the past that most of those in your audience respect. For example, a reference to the Bible or other holy books can often be quite effective. These volumes contain a wealth of material on almost any subject of importance. Note how effectively Martin Luther King, Jr., challenges the conscience of America by citing those authorities who framed the Constitution and the Declaration of Independence:

> When the architects of our Republic wrote the magnificent words of the Constitution and the Declaration of Independence, they were signing a promissory note to which every American was to fall heir. . . . It is obvious today that America has defaulted on this promissory note, insofar as her citizens of color are concerned. Instead of honoring this sacred obligation, America has given the Negro people a bad check; a check which has come back marked insufficient funds. However, we refuse to believe that there are insufficient funds in the great vaults of opportunity of this nation. And so we've come to cash this check, a check that will give us on demand the riches of freedom and the security of justice.

The use of testimony as a support is often less effective when dealing with a controversial subject. Anyone who has had anything to do with debate is aware that when you are dealing with a controversial subject of significance, there is sure to be an unlimited number of experts who disagree with one another.

Provided you have some expertise in regard to your subject, one of the best forms of testimony you can use is your own personal experience. If you have some background or experience in regard to your subject that qualifies you as somewhat of an expert, mention it in the introduction to your speech. Let your listeners know immediately that you are backing up the information you are giving them with your own "expert" testimony. If you wait until the middle or end of your speech to tell them about your background, chances are that some in your audience will think, "I didn't know the speaker was an expert on the subject. I guess I should have listened more carefully."

COMPARISON/CONTRAST

One of the basic principles of education is that the only way you can learn anything new is to be able to relate it to something you already know. Therefore, the best way to teach the unknown is to compare it to the known. Jesus used comparison very effectively when he preached to the different people he met. Depending upon the backgrounds and occupations of those in his audience at the time, he variously revealed what the kingdom of heaven is like by comparing it to: a fisherman throwing his net into the sea and pulling in both good fish and bad, a farmer harvesting his wheat along with weeds, a merchant selling all he had to buy a single pearl of great value, and ten bridesmaids who took their lamps and went to meet the bridegroom. This kind of comparison is called figurative comparison or analogy. It describes similarities between things that are otherwise different. Other examples are the comparison of a bargaining meeting to a barroom brawl and a major speech to a parachute jump without a parachute.

A literal comparison describes similarities between things that are physically alike. It can often give your listener a clear mental picture of what you are talking about. For instance, if you say that the new dean of men looks like a young Robert Redford or that a Trident submarine is half again as long as a football field, you are offering your listener a clear basis of comparison. Less visual examples would be comparisons between interest rates in the United States in 1985 and 1986, academic standards in private and public universities, and jazz versus rhythm and blues. Literal comparisons are often used to reinforce particular points of view. How many times have you heard or used an argument similar to the following: "Why can't I learn to drive? Sally already has her driver's license, and she's a year younger than I am"?

Comparing differences is often called contrast. When you compare high school and college, living at home or on your own, and apples and oranges, you are emphasizing differences rather than similarities between like things. Consider the comment, "Boy, you kids nowadays get away with murder. When I was your age I wouldn't dream of doing that." You are backing up your point of view by emphasizing differences rather than similarities.

VISUAL AIDS

When used effectively, visual aids can be an excellent means of reinforcing or clarifying your ideas. If, however, the visual aid is used incorrectly, it can detract from rather than improve your speech. Here are some specific suggestions for using visual aids:

1. A visual aid must be large enough to be seen by the entire audience. If you are using a poster or chart, make sure that your lettering or drawings are dark or vivid enough so that those farthest away will get the information. Unless each member of your audience can see your visual aid clearly, don't use it.

2. Avoid visual aids that are overly complex. A complicated drawing or too many words or statistics will defeat your purpose. A listener must be able to grasp the meaning of your visual instantly.

3. Your visual aid should clarify or reinforce your point. Displaying a picture of yourself holding a string of bass during a demonstration on how to fillet fish might do something for your ego but will add nothing to your audience's understanding.

4. Make sure that you maintain good eye contact when referring to your visual aid. It is for the audience, not you, to look at. Besides, looking out at your audience will help you determine if you are displaying your visual in a way that can easily be seen by all.

5. Whenever possible, use posterboard or a flip board rather than a chalkboard during your presentation. If you must use a chalkboard, avoid turning your back to the audience for an extended period. Limit your use of the board to a simple drawing or a few words or phrases, or put what you need on the board before you begin the speech.

6. Keep your visual aid out of sight except when you are using it. Attention is intermittent. A person pays attention to something for a while, stops for a moment or so, and goes back to paying attention again. If you leave an interesting visual aid out to look at, chances are that some in your audience might find themselves paying attention to it rather than your speech.

7. Include your visual aid when practicing your speech. Become so familiar with your visual aid that you can refer to any part of it with little loss of eye contact. Know where your aids will be when you want them and where you will put them when they are not being used.

8. Never pass a visual aid around through the audience. If you do, you will lose the attention of at least three listeners—the one looking at the aid,

the one who has just passed the aid on, and the one who will be getting the aid next. An exception would be if you were passing out an aid or handout to each member of your audience. There is less chance that this activity will be distracting if you pass the items out near the end of your speech, perhaps even at the conclusion.

9. Make sure that your visual aid does not take up too much time. Remember, you are using the visual aid to support a point you are making in your speech, not as a section of the speech itself. Running three minutes of a movie or slides during a five-minute speech is an overly long and inappropriate use of visual aids. On the other hand, make sure that everyone has enough time to see and understand your visual aid.

10. Do not let your visual aid interfere with the continuity of your speech. If, for example, you are going through the steps of mixing the ingredients of a cake or applying glaze to a ceramic during a speech to demonstrate, don't stop talking to your audience while doing so. Your visual aid must support what you are saying, not substitute for it.

COMBINED SUPPORTS

Often supporting materials are used in combination with one another. Thus you might support a point of view with comparative statistics, a visual aid that has to be explained, an example that includes expert testimony, and so on. Tests, experiments, studies, surveys, polls, programs, and investigations often involve a combination of supporting devices. For example, the benefits of an exercise program might be stated in terms of comparison, testimony, and statistics. An investigation into the effects of budget cuts on the poor might involve examples, testimony, comparison, and statistics. Or either might be explained to an audience with the help of a visual aid.

GATHERING SUPPORTING MATERIALS

If you have chosen a subject that you are interested in, you will quite likely find supporting material for your speech from your own personal experience. Of course you will often feel the need to supplement your own experience with additional facts and other points of view. This need should present no problem to you, provided you start early enough. There are two primary sources of information: (1) written sources (books, newspapers, magazines, and pamphlets) and (2) interviews. When gathering information, always remember to take careful notes which include the exact source of your information.

Written Materials

The best place to find written materials for your speech is at your college or community library. The card catalog lists all the books in the library under three headings: title, author, and subject. Periodical indexes list articles published in magazines and other periodicals according to subject. Of these indexes, the *Reader's Guide to Periodical Literature* is the most popular. A newspaper is an excellent source for up-to-date information. Your library will undoubtedly have back copies or microfilm of a number of newspapers. Some newspapers have indexes which list by subject the articles that have appeared in that paper. The *New York Times Index* lists the subject, date, page, and column of every article that has appeared in that paper since 1913. Finally, in the library reference room you will find almanacs, atlases, biographies, encyclopedias, and countless other reference books that will give you pertinent data on almost any topic. If you run into a problem, it is part of the librarian's job to help you solve it. Don't be afraid to ask for assistance.

Interviewing

An interview can be an effective and interesting way to gather information. Up-to-date information from an expert in the field can often carry a great deal of weight. Faculty members, clergy, community leaders, and local politicians are among many who would be pleased to provide you with speech material. Keep in mind, though, that no matter how expert the person you are interviewing is, you don't want to overload your speech with references to that interview. Unless you are an experienced note taker, you will want to tape record your interview. Most subjects will gladly give you permission to tape record them if you explain exactly what use of the material you wish to make.

TAKING NOTES

The more accurate your notes are, the less time you will have to spend rechecking your sources for dates, statistics, and exact wording.

Although you can record your material in notebooks or looseleaf folders, I find that the use of note cards is best. There are a number of reasons for this: (1) Note cards are easy to handle. If a note card contains information that you decide not to use, you can throw it away. (2) Note cards can be shuffled and used to organize the speech. (3) Note cards can easily be used for reference during the delivery of the speech or during the question-and-answer period following it. (4) Note cards can more easily be grouped and classified. Here are some suggestions to follow when taking your notes:

1. Use note cards that are uniform. Whether you buy them or make them yourself, note cards that are uniform in size and stiffness are easier to work with and store.

2. Record the exact source of your information. When the source is written, indicate the call number, author(s), title, date, and page numbers in case you want to refer to the source again. If your information came from an interview, indicate the time and date of the interview along with the interviewed person's name and credentials.

3. Keep notes brief. Don't copy large selections of material at random. Be selective. Spend time deciding exactly what you want to say before writing.

4. Be accurate. If you are copying a direct quotation, make sure that the wording is exact. If you are paraphrasing, make sure the paraphase accurately conveys the meaning of the original.

5. Indicate the subject of each note card. Then when you are ready to organize your speech, you can put the cards in piles according to the points they are supporting.

6. Take an ample number of notes. Don't be afraid of gathering too much information. It is much easier to select the best from an overabundance of information than to find you are short and have to go back and look for more.

EXERCISES

1. Choose one of the following statements or write one of your own and support it with examples, statistics, testimony, comparison/contrast, and explanation.

   "Gambling should be legalized in our state."
   "The U.S. should pass a law abolishing the death penalty."
   "The U.S. should adopt a system of national health care."

2. Indicate an authority your classmates would respect in the following fields: science, education, energy, medicine, law, football, baseball, and music.

3. Find an ad that combines two or more supporting devices to sell its prod-

uct. Do the supporting devices seem accurate and objective? Comment on whether you think the ad is effective and why or why not.

4. Answer the following questions about your school library.

    a. What hours is your library open?
    b. What is the name and title of the person in charge?
    c. What is the procedure for examining a periodical?
    d. What newspapers does your library subscribe to?
    e. For what period of time can a book be checked out?
    f. What fines are imposed for overdue books or records?

chapter five

PREPARING THE CONTENT OF YOUR SPEECH

Now that you have gathered the supporting materials you will need to reinforce or clarify your central idea and main points, you are ready to begin preparing the content of your speech. The content should be developed around the central-idea statement, which is the controlling idea of the speech. With a basic speech pattern you might simply state and support the central idea. Speeches of personal experience to entertain or to make a point are often developed in this statement-support pattern.

In the speech of personal experience to make a point, there are two possible approaches. (1) The central idea (the point) is stated at the beginning of the speech followed by a story that reinforces it. The story is told first, and the point is made at the conclusion of the speech. Thus you might say, "I learned at an early age never to trust strangers," and tell your audience about an experience you had that taught you this lesson, or you might relate the experience first and end by saying, "And that's how I learned never to trust strangers."

In most cases, however, the central idea of a speech quite naturally breaks up into two or three main points. For example, consider a speech with the central idea: Our school cafeteria is an excellent place to eat. You might support it with these three main points: (1) the prices are reasonable; (2) the food is well prepared; and (3) the surroundings are neat and clean. The basic format for this speech would be as follows:

INTRODUCTION   The introduction of a speech should capture the audience's attention, give them a reason for listening, indicate the central idea of the speech—for example, Our school cafeteria is an excellent place to eat—and preview the major points.

BODY   First main point—the prices are reasonable (supporting material).

Second main point—the food is well prepared (supporting material).

Third main point—the surroundings are neat and clean (supporting material).

CONCLUSION   The conclusion of a speech should end with a summary, a restatement of the central idea, a question, a call to action, or a vision of the future.

Although some central ideas can logically be broken down into five or more main points, it is advisable to limit your speech to no more than four. Keep in mind that you are speaking to listeners, who must assimilate and remember the information you are giving them. Few, if any, will be taking notes. If you have too many points, the chances are great that you will wind up confusing and perhaps even losing some of your audience.

ORGANIZING YOUR SPEECH

As you can see from the format above, a speech is divided into three parts—the introduction, the body, and the conclusion. Each of these parts has a particular function.

Introduction

An introduction should capture the attention of the audience, give them a reason for listening, and clearly state the central idea of the speech. In many cases a preview of the main ideas should be given. As a rule of thumb, the introduction should comprise only 10 to 15 percent of the total speech time.

Body

The body should comprise from 75 to 85 percent of the speech. That is where the speaker's message is presented. The body consists of the main points of the speech, along with the supporting materials necessary to develop each point, and clear transitions from each point to the next.

Conclusion

A conclusion should be short and to the point. It should comprise from 5 to 10 percent of the total speech and include one or any combination of the following: a summary of the main points, a restatement of the central idea, a question, a call to action, or a vision of the future.

PLANNING THE BODY

The body is the most important part of the speech. It contains the development of the central idea, the major points, and the supporting material that proves or clarifies the central idea and main points. Therefore, it is wise to develop the body of the speech first. There are four steps to follow as you plan the body of your speech:

1. Decide on the main points that will support or clarify your central idea.
2. Write these main points as complete sentences.
3. Arrange the central idea and main points in a logical organizational pattern.
4. Add appropriate supporting material to clarify and reinforce your central idea and main points.

Decide on Main Points

The central-idea statement you have chosen should determine the main points you select. The number of main points you need to put your ideas across is up to you. In some speeches, as you remember, the body may consist simply of the support you are using for your central idea. In others you might choose two to four main points around which to build your speech. Keep in mind during this stage that you are trying to get your audience to accept and remember your ideas. As I pointed out earlier, if you develop any more than four main points, chances are that some in your audience will be unable to remember them.

Write Your Main Points as Complete Sentences

Writing your main points as complete sentences will help you in determining whether they reinforce or clarify your central ideas effectively and whether they cover your subject adequately. Each main point should be stated clearly and succinctly so there is no doubt in your listeners' minds as to what your point is and what you are trying to accomplish. Following are four suggestions for developing main points for your speech:

1. They should clarify or reinforce your central idea.
2. They should cover your subject adequately.
3. They should be equal in importance.
4. They should be worded in a similar way.

They should reinforce or clarify your central idea.   In order to be effective, your main points must make your central idea clearer or more forceful. These main points will in turn be clarified or reinforced by your supporting materials: examples, illustrations, statistics, explanation, testimony, comparison/contrast, and visual aids. Main points that do not clearly reinforce or clarify your central idea are confusing. Consider the following example:

Central idea: Iguanas make great pets.

Main point: They are inexpensive.

Main point: They are clean.

Main point: They are easy to care for.

Main point: They are reptiles.

Note that while the first three main points reinforce the central idea that Iguanas make great pets, the fourth point, that they are reptiles, does not. While it can be argued that many reptiles make excellent pets, most would agree that others, like cobras, crocodiles, and dinosaurs, do not.

They should cover your subject adequately. In order to achieve your purpose in speaking, you must be sure to provide your listeners with the information they need to respond correctly. Choose your main points carefully so that they fully develop your central idea. It is always better to have too much material than to fail to cover a subject adequately. Remember, your success or failure as a speaker is largely dependent on audience response.

They should be equal in importance and parallel in phrasing. Besides reinforcing and clarifying your central idea, your main points should be equal in importance to each other. Supporting your central idea with two strong points and one weak one will lessen your effectiveness. You will find yourself devoting a considerable amount of time to two points and very little to the third. While you don't have to devote exactly the same amount of time to each point, they should be somewhat near the same length. Also, if you word your main points in a parallel manner, it will emphasize the fact that they are equal in importance. One way to insure similarity in phrasing is to repeat key words. Compare these two sets of main points for a speech on swimming.

Nonparallel

Central idea: Swimming is beneficial to your health.
Main point: It conditions your mind and your body.
Main point: You exercise most of your muscles.
Main point: The capacity of your lungs is increased.

Parallel

Central idea: Swimming is beneficial to your health.
Main point: It conditions your mind and your body.
Main point: It exercises most of your muscles.
Main point: It increases your lung capacity.

Arrange Central Idea and Main Points

The information that you are presenting to your audience must be organized in such a way that it makes sense to them and can be easily followed. There are a number of ways that you can organize the central idea and main points that you present in your speech. The six most basic organizational patterns follow:

1.   Chronological order. Many speeches lend themselves to development in a chronological order. In this pattern you relate a series of incidents or explain a process according to the order in which the incidents or steps in the process occur or have occurred—from first to last. You might analyze the development of rock and roll or demonstrate how to make lasagna.

Example   Central idea: There are four steps to follow when making lasagna.

a.   Step 1 involves preparing the meat sauce.
b.   Step 2 includes making and cooking the pasta.
c.   Step 3 involves preparing the three cheeses.
d.   Step 4 is layering the ingredients into baking dishes and baking the lasagna.

2.   General to specific. In a sense, a general-to-specific pattern is found in most speeches. The central idea, usually given in the introduction, is a general statement, and it is followed by a statement of the main points in less general terms. Finally, each of these main points is supported by specific details. The opposite of this would be a specific-to-general pattern, where the main points are given first and the central idea is stated in the conclusion.

Example A   Central idea: Betty White is an excellent speech teacher.

a.   She has established an excellent rapport with her students and made them enthusiastic about speech.
b.   She has demonstrated that she was a thorough knowledge of her subject along with sound teaching techniques.

c. She has been able to communicate her understanding of speech to the students and has helped them improve.

Example B

a. Betty White has established an excellent rapport with her students and made them enthusiastic about speech.
b. Betty White has demonstrated that she has a thorough knowledge of her subject along with sound teaching techniques.
c. Betty White has been able to communicate her understanding of speech to the students and has helped them to improve.

Concluding central idea: Therefore, Betty White is an excellent speech teacher.

3. Topical. Sometimes a pattern of arrangement is suggested by the topic itself. For instance, a discussion of music history might logically divide itself into four areas: preclassical, classical, romantic, and contemporary. Similarly, a discussion of a college or university might involve the board of directors, the administration, the faculty, and the student body.

Example Central idea: The development of music can be roughly divided into four broad areas.

a. The first is preclassical.
b. The second is classical.
c. The third is romantic.
d. The fourth is contemporary.

4. Spatial. A subject might fall quite naturally into a spatial arrangement. An analysis of education in different parts of the country, a demonstration on how to landscape the front of a house, and an explanation of how the body digests foods would lend themselves to this pattern of development.

Example   Central idea: Digestion, the process by which the body absorbs and utilizes food, takes place in three areas of the body.

a. Digestion begins in the mouth, where the food is ground into a semisolid mass.
b. Digestion continues in the stomach, where food becomes a mixed liquid.
c. Digestion is completed in the small intestines, where the final stage occurs.

5.   Cause and Effect. Although it can be used as an organizational pattern for speeches to entertain or inform, the cause-and-effect pattern is most often used for persuasive speeches. A typical example is that of a salesperson trying to convince a prospective customer that buying the product (cause) will result in all sorts of advantages (effect). Following is an outline of a student speech that utilizes the cause-and-effect pattern to describe the beneficial effects of jogging.

Example   Central idea: Jogging is the ideal exercise.

a. It conditions the body.
b. It removes unwanted fat.
c. It provides emotional balance.

6.   Problem-solution. Another organizational pattern that is most often employed in speeches to persuade is the problem-solution order. This speech usually begins with an introduction that states a problem as the central idea of the speech. The body of the speech is organized around the solution or solutions to the problem. Following is a sample outline of a typical problem-solution speech:

Example   Central idea: The amount of money that our student government will receive from outside sources this year has been cut in half, eliminating funding for many of our programs.

The solution to this problem is to hold a two-day bratwurst festival during the month of October, which will raise enough money to make up the difference.

7. Motivated Sequence. Monroe's motivated sequence is yet another organizational pattern. It was developed in the 1930's by the late Alan H. Monroe, a speech professor at Purdue University. It lists a five-step plan of action.

1. Capture the attention of the audience.
2. Indicate a need for the audience to listen.
3. Show how your proposal will satisfy that need.
4. Visualize what will happen if the plan is put into operation.
5. Indicate the action you wish your audience to take.

Example Central idea: Congress must pass a federal law requiring stiffer penalties for drunken driving.

1. Show pictures of fatal crashes involving drunk drivers. (step 1)
2. Cite statistics that emphasize the problem. (step 2)
3. Show how tougher laws have worked in other countries. (step 3)
4. Describe life without the menace of the drunken driver on the road. (step 4)
5. Tell those in your audience to sign your petition. (step 5)

Source: Douglas Ehninger, Bruce Gronbeck, Ray McKerrow, and Alan Monroe, *Principles and Types of Speech Communication*, 10th ed. (Glenview, Ill.: Scott, Foresman, 1986), p. 153.

Speeches that are well organized are clearer and therefore more effective. Using one of the organizational patterns given above will make it easier for those in your audience to understand and remember the information in your speech. You have undoubtedly come in contact with many of these organizational patterns before. That is because the mind is conditioned to organize chronologically, spatially, topically, logically, and from general to specific. Your chances of communicating effectively with your audience will be much greater if you use an organizational pattern that can easily be followed.

Add Appropriate Supporting Material

Supporting materials are necessary for clarifying or proving the points you make in the body of your speech. By themselves the major and subordinate points are really only the structure or skeleton of your speech. It is the quality and relevancy of the supports you choose that make your ideas clear, interesting, and acceptable to your audience. Following is an outline of the body of the speech whose central idea is, Our school cafeteria is an excellent place to eat, to which supporting materials have been added.

BODY OF SPEECH

I. The prices are reasonable.
    A. (Testimony) Sue Smith, cafeteria manager, has told me how pleased customers are with food prices.
    B. (Statistics/Comparison) A student senate survey has determined that area restaurants charge from 20 to 30 percent more for comparable meals.
    C. (Example) I took my friend Mike and his girlfriend, Debbie, to lunch at our cafeteria, and they couldn't believe how low the prices were.
    D. (Visual aid/comparison) Here is an enlargement of a typical breakfast menu from our school cafeteria. When you compare it with these enlarged menus from the two restaurants closest to the school, you can see that the cafeteria's prices are consistently lower.
II. The food is excellent.
    A. It is top quality.
        1. (Testimony) Mrs. Sarah Willis, who does the buying for the school cafeteria, has testified that only USDA choice meats and top-quality bakery and produce are purchased by her.
        2. (Explanation) Chef Werner Knautz, in charge of food preparation for the cafeteria, explains that all food is prepared by second- and third-year students of hotel and restaurant cooking under the watchful eye of their professors.
    B. It is well prepared.
        1. (Comparison/testimony) A recent article in the MATC *Times* quoted the governor, who recently toured the college, as saying the meal he ate in the cafeteria was as good as he has had in any school in Wisconsin.
        2. (Example/testimony) I recently took my mother-in-law to the school cafeteria for a birthday lunch. We had tacos and burritos, and my mother-in-law, who is Mexican, said she had never tasted any that were better.
III. The surroundings are neat and clean.
    A. The eating area is spotless.
        1. (Explanation) During serving hours cafeteria personnel are ever

present, wiping off tables and cleaning up spills. After closing, the entire area is scrubbed thoroughly.

2. (Example) Last semester I was having lunch in the cafeteria with a group of friends. As she was approaching our table, one of them tripped and dropped her whole tray of food onto the floor. Within minutes the entire mess was cleaned up by two cafeteria workers.

B. The kitchen is immaculate.

1. (Testimony/comparison) Amos Jackson, city health inspector, has stated that in his twenty-six years of inspecting area restaurants he has never found one with a cleaner kitchen.
2. (Explanation) The kitchen and everything in it is cleaned each evening after closing. Linda Smith, a cafeteria worker, has only one assignment, to see that the kitchen stays as clean as possible throughout the day.

TRANSITIONS

The body of the speech outlined above consists of main and supporting points, along with supporting material for each. However, in order to move your listeners smoothly from one point to the next, you must include transitions or links between each point. Transitions act like guideposts for your listeners. When you use words like *also* and *in addition* you indicate that your thinking is moving forward. Words like *on the other hand* and *conversely* indicate a reversal of direction. Imagine the following situation: An instructor walks into class and says to her students, "As you all know, you are scheduled to take your mid-semester exam in this course today. However . . ." The instructor pauses. An audible sigh of relief is heard throughout the room. The word "however" has caused the students to reverse their thinking. There will be no exam today.

Transitions will help to provide coherence to your speech so that your ideas flow smoothly from one point to the next. Following are a number of suggestions for providing coherence to your speech:

1. Use transitional words: Also, again, as a result, besides, but, conversely, however, in addition, in contrast, likewise, moreover, nevertheless, similarly, then, therefore, thus, yet.

2. Use enumerative signposts. "There are three main reasons: first . . . second . . . third . . ."
   "Point A is this: . . ."

3. Repeat key words.
   "Our nuclear buildup isn't defense. Our nuclear buildup is suicide."

4. Conclude your discussion of one point by introducing the next point.
   "This concludes the discussion of step 2, stripping. Next we will consider step 3, sanding."

5. Begin your discussion of a new point with a reference to the point you just finished discussing.
   "Now that we have finished our discussion of step 3, sanding, we are ready to move on to step 4, refinishing."

Keep in mind that, as a listener you are obliged to do whatever you can to make your ideas as clear and interesting to your listeners as possible. Using effective transitions in your speeches will help you achieve this goal.

EXERCISES

1. Write out a central-idea statement and two or more main points for one or more of the following subjects as your instructor directs.
   a. Restaurants
   b. Hobbies
   c. Sports
   d. Entertainment
   e. Politics
   f. Fitness

Speech Assignment

Relating a personal experience to entertain. Deliver a two-to-three-minute speech in which you tell your audience of a personal experience you had that they will find entertaining. Your story can be either entirely true, partly true, or fictitious. It can utilize humor, novelty, the familiar, the startling, the vital, conflict, or suspense to hold the attention of the audience. The important thing is that you describe the situation in enough detail to create a mental picture for your audience.

Delivery: Deliver this speech extemporaneously with no more than one note card. An audience will expect you to have almost total eye contact when talking about your own experiences. The more spontaneous and relaxed you are, the more your audience will enjoy your speech.

SUGGESTED SUBJECTS

1. Camping can be fun, for bears
2. My most embarrassing experience
3. A day I'll never forget
4. I learned to ski the hard way
5. My first date

chapter six

THE
INTRODUCTION
AND CONCLUSION

THE INTRODUCTION

Now that you have outlined the body of your speech, you are ready to begin developing your introduction. In most cases an introduction to a speech has three objectives: (1) it should capture the listener's attention; (2) it should give the audience a reason for listening; and (3) it should indicate the main idea of the speech and, if desirable, preview its main points. Keep in mind that although an introduction will often include all three of those elements, at times one or more of them may be omitted.

Besides fulfilling some or all of these objectives, an effective introduction should lead smoothly into the body of the speech. While the first objective of the introduction is to get the attention of the audience, that attention must be held throughout the speech, or communication will not have taken place. Following are ten methods for getting and holding the attention of your audience. Each is followed by a model.

Start Off with Humor

When I was preparing this speech, I was reminded of the story of the woman who called up the fire department and screamed, "Come quick! My house is on fire." And when the fireman on the other end of the line responded, "OK lady, but how do we get there?" she replied, "Don't you have that big red truck anymore?" Now that story is kind of silly, but there's also a certain amount of truth to it. It won't be long before fire departments will no longer have red trucks.

Now that science has found that pastel colors are considerably more visible than red, more and more fire departments are changing to yellow or lime-green vehicles. However, this is only one of many changes fire departments have made over the last ten years. Today I'm going to tell you about some of the most interesting of these changes. Some of them, you won't believe.

Begin with a Startling Statement

Even though the dosages would be microscopic, so that you couldn't even see them, if two pounds of plutonium could be evenly distributed among the world's population, each person on earth would receive a lethal dosage. We wouldn't need poison gas or neutron bombs, the Soviet SS-18 missile or the MX. All we would need is two pounds of plutonium. In spite of this alarming fact, if things continue at the present rate, the United States will be producing seventeen hundred tons of plutonium by the year

2000. Unless we can find more foolproof safeguards for handling the stuff, the Russians won't have to push a button to annihilate us. We will do the job ourselves.

Ask a Rhetorical Question

Do you know what your chances are of getting AIDS in your lifetime? Well, if you are not a member of a high-risk group and do not get involved sexually with a member of a high-risk group, your chances are one in one million. If you are a weekly ticket buyer, those are roughly your chances of being the winner of a state lottery, or put another way, your chances of dying from any other cause are considerably greater. However, AIDS is a disease that has attracted much attention, and there is not a great deal known about it. Today I am going to talk about the symptoms of AIDS, how it is transmitted, and what is being done to combat it.

Begin with a Statistic

According to a 1985 Justice Department report, your chances of being murdered in a lifetime are 1 in 133. (That is unless you are a black male. Then they are 1 in 21.) And if you make less than $3,000 per year the chances are at least 1 in 18 that you'll be assaulted, raped, or robbed at some time in your future. Not a very good outlook is it? What these statistics tell us is that we live in a violent society. What they also tell us is that our society is more violent for some than for others. What are the reasons for this? Well, the reasons are many. However, the first and most important reason is that our society is divided into two groups—the "haves" and the "have nots."

Refer to a Previous Speaker

I really enjoyed Sarah's speech on how to save money by buying generic. I had no idea of how many products were sold under the generic label. Some of the comparative prices she quoted were fantastic. What a simple way to save money, too. And who isn't interested in that? In my speech I'm going to show you how you can get the best return on the money you save through buying generic by investing in an IRA. Now you might be saying to yourself, "I'm too young to be thinking about an IRA." Well, if you listen to me for just a few minutes, I think you will agree that no matter what your age or income is, there is an IRA designed just for you.

Start with a Quotation

It was Edmond Burke who said, "The only thing necessary for the triumph of evil is for good men to do nothing." Those words are as true today as they were in the eighteenth century. Many "good" Americans have sat by during the past five years as the Reagan administration weakened the Civil Rights Commission, opposed the renewal of the Voting Rights Act, redirected the Justice Department to protect "white male privilege," given tax breaks to segregated schools, and created an economy that has doubled the poverty rolls and resulted in increasing the nation's mortality rate for the first time in twenty years. If you have done little or nothing as yet to stop this alarming trend, here are some specific things you can do.

Begin with a Brief Story

For as long as I can remember, I have loved to fish. We own a summer cottage on a chain of lakes, and because my father is a teacher, we spend the entire summer there. Although I always caught my share of fish, I never did better than my brothers until two years ago. That's when I got the book *Lunkers Love Nightcrawlers* for my birthday. Since then, my success with fishing has been phenomenal. It is no longer unusual for me to catch a limit of bass or walleyes after a full day of fishing. But the secret isn't in living on a lake and knowing where to fish. The secret lies in knowing how to fish with nightcrawlers effectively. This morning I'm going to pass on to you a few of the secrets I've learned from *Lunkers Love Nightcrawlers*, an amazing book.

Refer to the Familiar

It used to be that when someone came here to Chicago, they'd make some comment about the wind, Mrs. O'Leary's cow kicking over the lantern, Carl Sandberg's poem "Chicago," or the song by the same name that made Frank Sinatra even richer. Now, though, I'd be surprised if someone came here and didn't talk about McMahon, the Refrigerator, or those great Super Bowl champion Bears. Well, I'm going to talk about some super Bears but not the 1986 variety. I'm going to talk about the fabulous Bears teams of the late 1940s and early 1950s.

List a Series of Examples

On their way home from a family reunion a young couple and their infant son are killed in a head-on collision with a pickup truck that crosses the center line. Two weeks later, an eight-year-old girl is crippled for life by a car that jumps the curb, crashes through a fence, and veers into the yard where she is playing. The next day, after leaving a party, a teenage girl and her drunken boyfriend are thrown from his motorcycle and killed when he fails to negotiate a dangerous curve. What do these accidents have in common? They were all caused by drivers who were intoxicated. They are typical stories that appear in newspapers day after day in cities throughout our nation. And the greatest tragedy is that many of these kinds of accidents would never happen again if we could do one thing: find a way to get the drunk driver off the road.

Begin with a Definition

Many people think of child abuse as an injury to a child resulting from a physical or sexual act. However, this is only one form of abuse. Dr. C. Henry Kempe of the University of Colorado Medical Center, a recognized authority on child abuse, has defined a victim as "any child who receives nonaccidental injury or injuries as a result of acts or omissions on the part of his parents or guardians." That means that if a child is injured as a result of not being fed properly or because of being left unattended, the person responsible is as guilty as one who has inflicted physical violence on a child. Making people more aware of exactly what constitutes child abuse would help in dealing with the problem. It's time we brought child abuse out of the closet and into the spotlight where it belongs.

The list of suggestions given above for attention-getting introductions is by no means complete. Other methods include referring to a recent event or one that is soon to take place, a buildup of suspense, the use of a visual aid as part of the introduction, the use of novelty or the unusual, an introduction involving conflict, and establishing a common ground with the audience.

Choose your introduction carefully. It should be consistent with the purpose and the central idea of your speech. A humorous introduction to a serious speech would be a poor choice. Be aware that the introduction is the first thing your audience hears, and therefore it has much to do with the effectiveness of your speech.

THE CONCLUSION

Some people feel that the conclusion is the most important part of the speech. It is your last chance to achieve your purpose, and it signals your audience that your speech is ending. Plan your conclusion carefully. It is the final impression the audience will get of your speech, and it should leave them with a sense of completeness. It is no accident that many of the most memorable lines from speeches have occurred at or near the conclusion. Among them are the following:

"I know not what course others may take, but as for me; give me liberty, or give me death."

Patrick Henry

"That we here highly resolve that these dead shall not have died in vain—that this nation, under God, shall have a new birth of freedom—and that the government of the people, by the people, and for the people shall not perish from the earth."

Abraham Lincoln

"Ask not what your country can do for you but what you can do for your country."

John F. Kennedy

Finally, remember never to introduce new material in your conclusion. To do so will leave your audience with the impression that you failed to plan your speech carefully and added the new material as an afterthought, or that you left something out of your talk and remembered it just as you were about to close. Either way, you wind up with egg on your face. Following are five suggestions for effectively concluding your speech:

1.   End with a restatement of your central idea. A speech that has as its central idea, We must bring child abuse out of the closet and into the spotlight, might end this way:

Because there has been a steady increase in child abuse in the United States during the 1980s, because in some of our states the penalties are stiffer for abusing animals than for abusing children, and because many people are not aware of what does or does not constitute child abuse there must be an immediate and concerted effort made to address this problem—

through litigation, through communication, through education, and through cooperation. We must pull child abuse out of the darkness and put it into the spotlight so that we can see it for the evil that it is.

2. End with a summary of the main ideas developed in your speech. A speech with the central idea, Our school cafeteria is an excellent place to eat, might conclude this way:

I imagine that by now you've come to the conclusion that I'm sold on our cafeteria, and you're right. But I have good reasons. When I went to grade school and high school I took a bag lunch most of the time. Not that the food wasn't good at those schools; it was. My mom just did a super job with the sandwiches and all the rest. Then I got to our school, tried the cafeteria, and that was it. That's where I eat while I'm at school because the prices are reasonable, the food is excellent, and the surroundings are neat and clean.

3. End with a call to action. The speech that has as its central idea, We must get the drunk driver off the road, might end this way:

As I said earlier, I am not taking a pie-in-the-sky approach to this problem. Drunk drivers have been on the road since the horse-and-buggy days, and there will probably be some operating flying saucers while under the influence. However, in spite of the fact that our legislators are dragging their feet in passing tougher laws, in spite of the fact that there are too many loopholes in present laws, and in spite of the fact that in many cases law enforcement is neither uniform nor strict enough, MADD, Mothers Against Drunk Driving, has made a difference. Slowly but surely, laws are getting tougher, the loopholes are being plugged, and enforcement is getting stricter and more uniform. By supporting MADD, you will be helping to get the drunk driver off the road. For as little as five dollars per year you can become a sustaining member. Pick up a membership blank from me at the end of our meeting today. Then, send it in along with your check or money order. The life you save may be your own or that of a loved one.

4. End with a rhetorical question. A speech with the central idea, We need foolproof safeguards for stockpiling and handling plutonium, might end this way:

Can the United States afford to manufacture and store a substance that is so deadly that a few ounces of it could destroy every living creature on this continent? The answer is obvious. However, our government has not yet responded. Haven't we learned anything from the space-shuttle tragedy? How many more will have to die before we set up failsafe systems? Write your representatives in the House and Senate now and tell them that we need foolproof safeguards for stockpiling and handling plutonium.

5. End with a positive vision of the future. The vision of the future that you project can be either positive or negative. The choice is up to you. For instance, in a problem-solution speech, you can visualize for your audience what the future will be like once the problem is solved. In the following excerpt is the positive vision of the future envisioned by Dr. Martin Luther King Jr. in his stirring speech ''I have a Dream.''

From every mountainside let freedom ring. And when this happens, and when we allow freedom to ring, when we let it ring from every village and every hamlet, from every state and every city, we will be able to speed up that day when all of God's children, black men and white men, Jews and gentiles, Protestants and Catholics, will be able to join hands and sing in the words of the old Negro spiritual, free at last. Free at last. Thank God almighty, we are free at last!

6. End with a negative vision of the future. There may be times when you will want to leave your audience with the feeling that the problem must be solved before it is too late. In these cases you might want to paint a picture of what the future will be like if something is not done to solve the problem as soon as possible. A speech with the central idea, Can the lower-income American family survive? might end with the negative vision of the future:

Unless we reverse the rising tide of poverty in this country, millions of families will disintegrate, not just break up. Child abuse and violence in the home will become epidemic as parents turn to alcohol and drugs to escape their problems and then return home to physically release their anger on their children or each other. Others who can't make it will place their children in foster homes or institutions or just simply abandon them. The potential for having the whole support system for families collapse is very real. We're seeing it now, and unless we do something about it very soon, the answer to the question I asked at the beginning of this speech, Can the lower-income American family survive? will be a tragic but resounding no!

OUTLINING THE SPEECH

Once you have developed the introduction, body, and conclusion of your speech, you should organize it in a complete-sentence outline form. This will enable you to see at a glance whether your central idea, main points, and subpoints are arranged in a clear and orderly manner. It will also help you to determine whether or not you have selected a sufficient and well-balanced assortment of the six kinds of supporting materials. Following is a model complete-sentence outline of a student speech on the benefits of walking:

Purpose: To persuade my listeners that walking is the perfect exercise

Organizational pattern: Cause and effect

INTRODUCTION

  I. (Testimony) Over 2000 years ago Hippocrates, the father of medicine said, "Walking is man's best medicine."
 II. (Explanation) Many feel that with heart disease the number one killer in the country and with over one-fourth of the population significantly overweight, exercise is the only answer.
III. (Testimony) The National Institute of Health says, "Walking is the most efficient form of exercise and the only one you can safely follow all the years of your life."
 IV. (Explanation) Everyone can walk, the young and old, sick and healthy, male and female.
     A. (Example) At the age of seventy, Elmer Orstatt, carrying a heavy backpack, walked from Georgia to Maine.
     B. (Example) Our retired neighbor and his wife walk five miles a day along with their eight-year-old grandson.
  V. (Central-idea statement) Walking is the ideal exercise because it strengthens the heart and conditions a person both mentally and physically.
      (Transition: The first, and probably most important thing that walking does, is to strengthen the heart.)

BODY

I. Walking strengthens the heart.
  A. It improves collateral circulation.
    1. (Explanation-visual aid) When some arteries become narrowed by fatty deposits, those nearby get wider and open up new branches to maintain an adequate blood supply.
    2. (Testimony) Dr. Samuel Fox, president of the American College of Cardiology says walking increases the number and size of your blood vessels and the efficiency of the heart.
    3. (Example) Steve McKanic was told at the age of forty-six that his heart condition was incurable and there was no hope. He started walking, and five years later he's active and healthy again.
    4. (Statistic) It is estimated that twelve million people in this country are being treated for heart disease and twelve million more have it and don't know it.
  B. It lowers blood pressure.
    1. (Explanation-visual aid) Muscles in your feet, calves, thighs, buttocks, and abdomen help push seventy-two thousand quarts of blood through your system every twenty-four hours. These muscles are exercised by walking, making them more efficient and thus lowering your blood pressure.
    2. (Example) Natalie Smith had such high blood pressure her doctor was afraid to let her drive a car because he thought she would have a stroke. She started walking, and a year later her blood pressure was normal.
    3. (Testimony) A recent study by Dr. Kenneth Cooper, author of *Aerobics*, demonstrates the connection between a person's fitness level and high blood pressure.
    4. (Example) Eula Weaver suffered her first high-blood-pressure-related heart attack at age seventy-eight. Today at eighty-nine she walks regularly, and her blood pressure is normal.
       (Transition: Second, walking helps to condition a person mentally by reducing stress and improving self-image.)
II. Walking conditions a person mentally.
  A. It reduces stress.
    1. (Testimony-comparison) Dr. Herbert DeVries, University of California physiologist, concluded after a university study that a fifteen-minute walk reduced neuromuscular tension more effectively than a standard dose of tranquilizers.
    2. (Example) Albert Einstein, Harry Truman, and Abraham Lincoln walked daily to escape from the tension of their jobs.

3. (Testimony) Dr. Paula Dudley White, dean of American cardiologists, said, ''A minimum of an hour a day of fast walking is absolutely necessary for one's optimal health, including that of the brain.''
4. (Testimony-comparison) Dr. Hans Selye's well-known experiment on the effects of psychological stress on sedentary and active rats demonstrates the effectiveness of physical conditioning in combating stress.

B. It improves self-image.
1. (Testimony) After a company-sponsored program of walking for twenty minutes twice daily, the thirty women involved said they felt better, happier, and more productive.
2. (Testimony) ''Walking,'' says psychologist John Martin, ''helps you function more efficiently because you know you are doing something positive and constructive, and this makes you feel better about yourself.''
3. (Example) Aunt Rose, who has tried unsuccessfully to lose weight for years, started walking and in nine months went from a size 22 to size 14. She is a new person.
4. (Explanation) Walking improves circulation, sending more oxygen to the brain and creating a euphoria that improves self-concept.
   (Transition: Finally, walking conditions a person physically by aiding in weight control and improving physical fitness.)

III. Walking conditions a person physically.
A. It removes unwanted fat.
1. (Visual aid) This chart indicates the number of calories a person of a particular weight will expend in an hour by walking between two and five miles per hour.
2. (Statistical testimony) Dr. Charles T. Kuntzleman, national fitness consultant to the YMCA, estimates that there are presently fifty million Americans who are seriously obese.
3. (Example) Three-hundred-pound Molly Ryan, who claimed to have a glandular problem that kept her fat, began walking after a heart attack and lost one hundred pounds after the first year.
4. (Comparison) Time-and-motion studies indicate that the typical overweight person walks 2.8 miles per day, compared to 4.8 miles per day for a person of normal weight.

B. It improves a person's fitness.
1. (Testimony) Dr. Lawrence Golding conducted a controlled experiment with twenty-five women at Kent State University in which he found that walking combined with dieting was far superior to dieting alone in its effect on physical fitness.

2. (Comparison) A study of the health records of thirty-one thousand double-decker-bus workers in London found that the fare collectors, who walked around the bus and climbed the stairs regularly, had a much lower mortality rate and faster recovery from heart attacks than the inactive bus drivers.
3. (Example) Scrambling over the slopes of their mountainous homeland has given the long-lived citizens of Hunza in the Himalayas such a high degree of cardiovascular fitness that even when they get a heart attack, it does little harm.
4. (Visual aid) This chart, devised by the Michigan Heart Association, will help you determine whether or not lack of fitness is increasing your chances of having a heart attack.

    (Transition: You have heard about the benefits of walking for the young or old, male or female, and sick or healthy. All you really need for this exercise program are your two feet.)

CONCLUSION

I. (Explanation) It is obvious that exercise is necessary to add years to your life and life to your years.
II. (Comparison) It doesn't matter which exercise you use as long as it moves you into the good or excellent fitness category.
III. (Explanation) Walking is the easiest and most efficient way for anyone to get fit and stay fit and everyone can use it.
IV. (Explanation) Walking is an exercise that will strengthen your heart and improve both your mental and physical fitness.

BIBLIOGRAPHY

Books:
Allsen, P. E. and Harrison, J. M. *Fitness For Life*. Dubuque, Iowa: William C. Brown, 1976.
Kuntzleman, Charles T. *The Complete Book of Walking*. New York: Simon & Schuster, 1978.
Man, John. *Walk!* New York: Paddington Press Ltd., 1979.
Periodicals:
Conniff, J. C. "Getting on a Good Footing." *New York Times Magazine*, April 23, 1978.
Goldstein, J. "Walkers of the World, Unite!" *Fitness for Living*, May/June 1986.
Howorth, D. "The Art of Walking." *Consumer Bulletin*, April 1978.
McDermott, B. "Going Through Life at a Walk." *Sports Illustrated*, May 8, 1978.

Although an outline for your speech similar to the one above involves a great deal of preparation, it is important for a number of reasons. First, it provides a logical arrangement of your main and subpoints along with an idea of the supporting materials you are going to use. This will enable you to determine whether your ideas flow smoothly from one to another, and whether you have included a well-balanced and sufficient number of the six kinds of supporting materials. Second, it will provide a framework from which you can prepare note cards or a phrase outline, or from which you can write out a speech to be delivered from manuscript or from memory.

The outline above includes a bibliography. While many of the speeches you deliver will involve your own experience, there are times when you will want to include materials you have gathered through research. In these cases, or whenever your instructor so directs, attach a bibliography to your preparation outline.

EXERCISES

1. Develop alternative introductions for an upcoming speech using the suggestions given in this chapter for getting and holding the attention of your audience.
2. Develop alternative conclusions for an upcoming speech using the suggestions given in this chapter for successfully concluding your speech.
3. Write out a complete-sentence outline for an upcoming speech.

Speech Assignment

Relating a personal experience to make a point. Develop a two-to-three-minute speech in which you tell your audience of an experience you had that taught you a lesson. The story may be true, partly true, or fictitious. Develop your material informally with emphasis on details of action.

Delivery. This speech should be delivered extemporaneously. Use no more than one note card. An audience will expect you to have almost total eye contact when telling of your own experiences.

Sample Central Ideas

1. Taking a chance can pay off.
2. A first-aid course can save someone.
3. Seatbelts save lives.
4. Don't judge a person on the basis of your first meeting.

chapter seven

PREPARING FOR DELIVERY

After you have finished organizing the content of your speech, you are ready to prepare it for delivery. The manner in which you prepare your speech will depend on the method of delivery you choose. Impromptu speeches (those delivered on the spur of the moment) are either not prepared at all or prepared very hastily. Manuscript speeches are written out completely. Memorized speeches are usually written first and then committed to memory. The extemporaneous speech is carefully prepared but delivered without having been written out or memorized. In most situations it is by far the best method of delivery. Besides providing spontaneity, it will enable you to adapt the message to your audience as you are speaking to them and to modify it in response to their feedback.

You have a number of options available to you when you choose to speak extemporaneously. The two most common of these are (1) develop a delivery outline of key words and phrases from your complete-sentence outline and deliver the speech from it, or (2) formulate note cards containing key words from your complete-sentence outline and deliver the speech from them. Following is a sample delivery outline made from the complete-sentence outline on pages 67–70. At first glance it may appear to have little meaning. Keep in mind, however, that it is meaningful to the speaker and provides signals as to the structure, the ideas, and the direction of the speech.

THE DELIVERY OUTLINE

I. Over 2000, Hippocrates
II. Heart disease #1
III. NIH—most efficient
IV. Everyone can
    A. E. Orstatt
    B. Neighbors
V. (Central idea) Strengthens heart, conditions mentally, physically (The first . . . strengthens)

BODY

I. Strengthens heart
    A. Collateral circulation
        1. Wider—new branches
        2. Dr. Fox—number, size
        3. Steve McKanic
        4. 12 million know/don't

   B. Blood pressure
       1. Visual aid
       2. Nathalie Smith
       3. Cooper—fitness—HBP
       4. Eula Weaver
(Secondly . . . stress, self-image)
 II. Conditions mentally
   A. Reduces stress
       1. Dr. deVries—neuromuscular tension
       2. Einstein, Truman, Lincoln
       3. Dr. White—1 hour—brain
       4. Dr. Selyes—rats
   B. Improves image
       1. 30 women
       2. Dr. Martin (read quote)
       3. Aunt Rose (22–14)
       4. Oxygen—euphoria
(Finally . . . physically)
III. Conditions physically
   A. Unwanted fat
       1. Visual aid
       2. Dr. Kuntzleman—50 million
       3. Molly Ryan (100 lbs)
       4. TM studies (2.8–4.8)
   B. Fitness
       1. Dr. Golding (25 women)
       2. 31,000 bus workers
       3. Hunza in Himalayas
       4. Visual aid
(You have heard . . .)

CONCLUSION

   I. Years to life/life to years
  II. Doesn't matter which
 III. Easiest, most efficient, everyone
 IV. Strengthens mentally, physically

USING NOTE CARDS

Many extemporaneous speakers choose to deliver their speeches from note cards rather than from a delivery outline. There are several advantages to using note cards. Note cards are easier to handle than a sheet of paper, and they are less noticeable. They won't waver if your hand trembles slightly. Note cards are especially helpful if you must deliver your speech without a lectern. You can hold the cards in one hand and still be able to gesture freely. Here are a number of suggestions to follow when using note cards:

1. Use standard three-by-five-, four-by-six-, or five-by-eight-inch note cards. The number of cards you use will depend on the length and complexity of your speech. If you choose to make your own cards rather than buy them, use rigid paper or cardboard.

2. Always use note cards as unobtrusively as possible except when reading a direct quotation or complicated statistics. In these cases hold your notes up so that your audience can see you are taking special care to be accurate.

3. Make sure your notes are legible. Note cards are easy to read when they are typed or printed in capital letters and double or triple spaced.

4. Number multiple note cards. That way you will be able to put them in order quickly if you happen to drop them or find they are disarranged.

5. Write on only one side of your note card. Even though your audience will expect you to use notes when delivering your speech, turning the cards over is distracting and time consuming.

6. Avoid writing your notes in too much detail. Note cards should serve only as a guide when delivering your speech. The extemporaneous method requires good eye contact and spontaneity. Overly detailed notes might tempt you to read your speech.

7. Avoid putting too much down on each card. Except for cards on which you have written full quotations or a set of statistics, limit to five the number of lines you put on a card. That way you'll be able to find your place in an instant. Remember, except for direct quotations and complicated statistics, the notes are there to jog your memory. Longer speeches will just require more cards.

8. Highlight ideas you wish to stress. Circle or underline key words so that you will remember to emphasize them while delivering your speech. It is often helpful to make notations on your note cards to ''pause'' or ''slow down'' at different times during your speech.

Here is a sample note card, which could be used to substitute for a section of the delivery outline above. It begins with the transition from the introduction to the body of the speech. Note that although the wording is similar to the key-word outline, the symbols of outlining, Roman numerals, capital letters and so on are left out.

---

(3)

(THE FIRST . . . STRENGTHENS)

COLLATERAL CIRCULATION—WIDER—NEW BRANCHES

Dr. FOX (NUMBER—SIZE) STEVEN McKANIK

12 MILLION   KNOW/DON'T   VISUAL AID

THE MANUSCRIPT

If you choose to deliver your speech from manuscript or memory, you must write it out completely in the same way you would word it if you were delivering it extemporaneously. In a written speech as in an extemporaneous one, to be effective you must use language that is clear, interesting, and appropriate.

Clarity

While clarity is important in all communication, it is indispensible to speech. A reader can reread a passage as many times as necessary to understand it. For the listener it must be instantly understood or it is gone. If too much of what you say is missed or misinterpreted, your communication will fail. You can achieve clarity in speaking by (1) using an oral style, (2) choosing concrete rather than abstract words, and (3) using specific rather than general words.

Oral style   It is not unusual for beginning speakers to deliver manuscript or memorized speeches that are unclear because they sound stilted or unnatural. This is usually because these speakers have composed them in a written rather than an oral style. While there are similarities between the two styles, there are also significant differences. For this reason, whenever you write a speech always read it aloud as you are writing to make sure that it sounds like you talking in a conversational way. Following are some of the most common characteristics of an oral style:

1. An oral style is replete with contractions. Although in writing, *will not* and *it is* are often preferred to the contractions *won't* and *it's*, contractions are common to an oral style.

2. Oral sentences are usually shorter and less complex than written sentences. Your English teachers insisted that you use longer and more complex sentences in your writing to achieve variety. However, variety can be achieved nonverbally in speech, and overly long sentences cause problems for both speakers and listeners.

3. Oral sentences usually employ a subject-verb order. A common method for achieving variety in writing is to combine normal, periodic, parallel, and balanced sentences. In speaking, the normal sentence (subject-verb pattern) occurs far more frequently than any other type.

4. An oral style uses many familiar words. Always remember that when you are communicating your ideas, you must choose words that mean the same things to your listeners as they do to you. In most cases the best language to use in speaking is the simplest and most familiar.

5. An oral style makes frequent use of personal pronouns. The use of *us*, *we*, *our*, *you*, and *I* is typical of what is called a conversational speech style. They give the speech an air of familiarity, as if the speaker is talking "with" the audience rather than "to" them.

Concrete Words   Concrete words refer to specific objects or particular instances, things that are relatively easy to visualize or define. They differ from abstract words, which refer to concepts, ideas, or emotions and often mean different things to different people. *Dog, book, rose, World War II,* and *Easter* are concrete words. *Democracy, communism, love,* and *hate* are abstract words. Obviously, a concrete word will always be clearer to your audience than an abstract one. Whenever possible, choose concrete rather than abstract words for your speech. When you must use abstract terms, define them as clearly and completely as you can.

Specific Words   Another way to achieve clarity in your speaking is to choose specific rather than general words. General words refer to a group or class of things. Specific words refer to a particular part of that group. Specific words are always clearer. Imagine going to your favorite butcher shop and asking for two pounds of meat. How can the butcher fill your order without knowing what kind of meat you want? Two pounds of beef is better but still not specific enough. Do you want hamburger, ground chuck, rib roast, pot roast, or eye of round? Even if you say steak, you leave the butcher wondering which one of a dozen or more kinds of steak you mean. When wording your speech, do your audience and yourself a favor and be as specific as you can.

Interest

An effective way to make your speeches more interesting is to use words that appeal to any of the five senses: sight, hearing, taste, touch, and smell.

For example, while it might be perfectly accurate to tell your listeners that a man came toward you, it would be much more visual and therefore more interesting to them if you told them that he staggered, lurched, inched, or crawled. In the same manner, the "eager buzz" of excited fans at a homecoming game and the spicy red chili that heats the mouth and causes perspiration to rise from the pores of the brow present vivid images to those listeners who can relate to them through one or more of their senses.

A second way of adding interest to your speeches is to use descriptive language to present a clear and definite word picture of what is taking place. Note the following two statements: (1) I sat next to a pretty blonde. (2) I sat next to a tall, slender, tanned blonde with a round and radiant face and dark, inviting eyes. Which statement is more likely to hold attention and establish a clear mental picture?

A third way to make your speeches interesting is to use an attention-getting technique called the *real*—talking in terms of actual people and places. This technique involves giving names to the characters you describe in your stories. For example, it is easier to imagine yourself sitting next to "Sheldon" or "Juanita" than next to your "friend." One can more easily picture your being attacked by the neighbor's vicious boxer, Cruncher, than by the "dog next door."

Finally, you can make your speeches interesting by using the active rather than the passive voice. An added benefit is that besides being more vigorous, the active voice is usually less wordy. Note the following examples:

Passive. First, the water was boiled by Jane, and then the eggs were added. (13 words)

Active. Jane boiled the water first and then added the eggs. (10 words)

Passive. The rapist was shot by the intended victim (8 words)

Active. The intended victim shot the rapist. (6 words)

Appropriateness

When presenting your speech, you must always use language appropriate to your audience and the occasion. It would obviously be inappropriate to use sophisticated scientific terminology in explaining the problems faced in rocket liftoff to a group of laypeople. Not so obvious would be the use of electrical terms (even though simple) in a demonstration speech to a general audience on how to install a 220 outlet.

Unless you know your audience extremely well and the occasion warrants it, it is best to avoid off-color stories or profanity. Always keep in mind that you are speaking to a captive audience. While you might capture the attention of some in your audience with the startling use of a four-letter word or ribald story, any advantage you gain will be negated if you make others uncomfortable or antagonized.

Finally, except in cases where you make it obvious that you are deviating for a special effect, always observe the rules of correct grammar. An audience will forgive or even miss an occasional slip, but if your speech contains too many errors it will affect your credibility. Like it or not, one variable by which an audience tends to judge the competence of speakers is by their correct or incorrect use of language.

WRITING AND REVISING YOUR SPEECH

While an extemporaneous speech is carefully prepared in a full-sentence outline form, and the central idea, main points, and subpoints are carefully phrased, the rest of the speech is worded by the speaker as the speech is being presented. While the speaker is aware of the speech structure, it is not delivered word for word in a predetermined way.

On the other hand, the manuscript is carefully written by hand or typed and is read to the audience by the speaker. Memorized speeches are usually written in manuscript form before being committed to memory. Following are some suggestions for preparing a manuscript speech:

1. Set aside an adequate block of time in which to write your manuscript. It would be best if you could write out the entire speech in rough form during this first draft. Remember, you will be revising your material later.

2. Write your first draft as soon as possible after you have finished your preparation outline. This will allow as much time as possible for revising and rewriting.

3. When writing the rough draft of your manuscript, skip every other line and leave ample margins. You need room on the page to make additions or changes when you revise.

4. Write your speech as if you were talking to friends. When you have written a few sentences, read them aloud to make sure they sound like one person talking to another.

5. If you experience trouble writing in an oral style, try delivering your speech into a tape recorder from your preparation outline. Then copy what you have said from the recording. During your revision and rewrite, you can eliminate any awkwardness or repetition.

6. Don't be afraid of writing too much for your first draft. Be aware that it is easier to delete than to add material.

7. Allow a cooling-off period of at least twenty-four hours before you revise and rewrite the first draft of your manuscript. Before considering any changes, read your manuscript aloud to get an overall impression of it.

8. A manuscript speech should have a specific form. Guidelines for this form might be given to you by your instructor. The following are typical:

   a. A manuscript should be divided into three parts—the introduction, the body, and the conclusion.
   b. A manuscript should be typed or printed (double or triple spaced) on only one side of the paper.
   c. A manuscript must be legible at a glance. Never write out a manuscript longhand. Consider typing or printing it in caps. Underline or circle important parts.
   d. Multiple pages of a manuscript should be numbered, and the pages should be loose rather than stapled together.
   e. A manuscript should be neat in appearance, punctuated correctly, and free from grammatical errors, misspelled words, and awkward sentences.

PRACTICING THE SPEECH

Regardless of whether you deliver your speech extemporaneously, from manuscript, or from memory, the key to doing so effectively is practice. Here are some suggestions for practicing your speeches:

1. Allow ample time for practice. Practice delivering your speech from two to five times. The idea is to practice enough to develop an easy and natural delivery but not to the extent that you unintentionally memorize an extemporaneous or manuscript speech.

2. Always practice with the same key-word outline, note cards, or manuscript that you plan to use when delivering your speech. If you retype something, run it through a practice session to make sure you haven't typed in an error or left something out.

3. Always practice your speech as if you were delivering it to your intended audience. After you have practiced alone a few times, try to find a person or two to serve as your audience.

4. Go through the entire speech during each practice. If you hit a trouble spot or two during practice, don't stop and start over. Chances are that if you do, you might do this while delivering your speech. Like it or not, the actual delivery of the speech is more stressful than practice. Don't give yourself any unnecessary handicaps.

5. Do not try to deliver your speech the same way each time you practice it. Whether your speech is extemporaneous, manuscript, or memorized, an important characteristic is spontaneity. Delivering an extemporaneous speech the same way each time might cause you to unintentionally memorize the words. Delivering a manuscript or memorized speech the same way each time could inhibit your vocal variety.

6. Do not coordinate specific gestures with the exact wording of your speech. To be effective, gestures must be spontaneous. While you should practice your speech with the kinds of emphatic and descriptive gestures you will be using in its delivery, don't pinpoint the exact moment to raise your index finger or dust off your shoulder during a speech. A planned or stilted gesture is worse than no gesture at all.

7. Practice your speech aloud with the same volume you plan to use in delivering it. Don't go over the speech in your head or say it so softly that no one can hear you.

8. Practice your speech each time with whatever visual aids you plan to use. If you plan to mix some ingredients together during your speech, mix them during at least one practice session. This will help prevent slipups.

9. Time your speech in practice. No one appreciates a speech that goes on and on interminably. If you have been given a specific time limit for your speech, conform to it while practicing. As a safeguard, arrange for a friend in the audience to signal you when you have only one minute or so left.

10. Practice the way you will approach the speaker's stand at the beginning of the speech and leave it at the conclusion.

11. If you have access to a tape or video recorder, use it. Recorders are excellent aids. The best audience you can have is you, provided you have learned to listen to yourself critically and objectively.

12. If possible, try to practice at least once in the room where you will be delivering your speech or a similar room. Anything you can do in practice to approximate the real thing is worth the effort.

STAGE FRIGHT

It was Shakespeare who told us that all the world is a stage and that we are all actors on that stage. Whether or not you agree with that metaphor about life, it seems to fit the speech situation aptly. There is a certain amount of acting involved in delivering a speech. In fact, one can almost visualize a spotlight on the speaker. From the moment you begin to walk up to the speaker's platform until the time you sit down after finishing your speech you are the center of attention for your audience. It is no wonder then that many speakers, both beginning and experienced, feel a little nervous about getting up and delivering a speech. They are afflicted by stage fright—the fear that they will not do as well as they would like to in front of the audience. The symptoms of stage fright can be any one or a combination of the following: rapid pulse, shortness of breath, quivering voice, dry mouth, sweaty palms, or weak knees. Obviously, these symptoms can create a problem for a speaker. There are two things you can do to overcome this potential problem: (1) become familiar with the causes of stage fright and (2) use specific techniques to control anxiety.

Causes of Stage Fright

When you deliver a speech in class, you are communicating in a friendly atmosphere. You are speaking to fellow students who can empathize with you because they are in the same situation you are in. Under these circumstances a speaker should feel relaxed and at ease—but many don't. Why? The reason is that many beginning speakers see the situation as threatening rather than friendly. They worry that their classmates will see their shortcomings and imperfections, real or imaginary. Worrying too much about what other people will think of you can cause stage fright.

This is not to say, however, that you should not be concerned with what your listeners will think of your speech. You have good reason to be nervous if you deliver a speech that you have done little to prepare or practice. While most listeners will expect you to make mistakes while delivering your speech, especially if you are a beginning speaker, few will react favorably to your presentation if they feel it has involved little effort on your part. It is not hard to understand why those who are poorly prepared suffer from stage fright.

Stage fright can also occur when there is risk involved in a situation. Even professionals get the jitters on opening night, when the critics are in the audience. Students who find it easy to speak in a sociology or economics class might freeze up in a speech class because the instructor is evaluating their performance. You might, for example, have no difficulty communicating with your boss until you ask for that raise.

Finally, stage fright can be caused by a speaker's mental or physical health. Suppose a speaker is in a depressed mood because things are not going well at home or elsewhere. Consider the effect of a migraine headache or lack of sleep on a speaker's delivery. No matter how eager one might be to deliver the perfect speech, the importance of mental or physical health cannot be discounted.

How to Control Anxiety

Most speakers experience some anxiety when speaking before an audience. Since you probably will too, here are some specific suggestions for controlling stage fright:

1. Develop a positive mental attitude about speaking. Keep in mind that it is natural to be nervous about doing anything important. As you get more practice in speechmaking, you will find that this nervous energy can be transferred into vitalizing your speech.

2. Be alert both mentally and physically. Make sure that you are well rested on the day of your speech. If you are planning a party or have an exam to study for, choose a night other than the one before your speech.

3. Prepare your speech carefully. One of the best ways to avoid anxiety about your speech is to do such a thorough job of preparing it that you are anxious to deliver it.

4. Develop an attention-getting introduction. An effective way to start off with a positive attitude about your speech is to plan an imaginative introduction that will capture the immediate attention of your audience.

5. Practice your speech adequately. Once you have attained the proper degree of fluency, you will begin looking forward to delivering your speech.

6. Make sure your speech is audience centered. If you have developed a speech that you feel your audience will find interesting or useful, chances are that your concern will shift from yourself to the ideas you are trying to communicate.

7. Give yourself a peptalk before speaking. Bolster your self-confidence by saying to yourself, "I'll do a good job!" "I am well prepared!" "My audience will enjoy this!"

8. Go through a few relaxing exercises prior to speaking. Stretch your arms and legs; breathe deeply through the nose and exhale through the mouth; and yawn a few times to relax the throat muscles.

9. Look for friendly faces in the audience. There are always some in an audience who are more attentive than others. Search for these faces. They will provide you with positive feedback and help you to relax.

10. Listen carefully to the speakers who precede you. If you can relate something in your speech to a speech that was delivered earlier, you will demonstrate to your audience that you have the ability to think on your feet.

EXERCISES

Speech Assignments

1. *Reading a commercial.* Read a one-minute radio or TV commercial that you have written yourself or picked up from a local broadcaster. Study it carefully to decide how to best indicate meaning. Practice it so that you can deliver it easily and naturally.

Delivery: The job of the reader is to communicate sincerity and enthusiasm in an interesting way. You can do this best by using conversational style. Be yourself.

2. *Reading poetry.* Select poetry that falls within a one-to-two-minute time limit. Pick something you think your listeners will like and that you can handle intelligently. Study it carefully in regard to mood and purpose. Practice it so that you can read it effectively.

Delivery: Speak clearly and distinctly using variations in pitch, volume, rate, and inflection to make your reading interesting. Know your selection well enough so that you can maintain adequate eye contact.

3. *Reading prose.* Select a piece of prose that falls within a one-to-two-minute time limit. Pick something you think your listeners will like and that you can handle intelligently. Study it carefully in regard to mood and purpose. Practice it so that you can read it effectively.

Delivery: Speak clearly and distinctly using variations in pitch, volume, rate, and inflection to make your reading interesting. Know your selection well enough so that you can maintain adequate eye contact.

chapter eight

DELIVERY

Once you have determined your purpose and subject, analyzed your audience, developed the content of your speech, prepared it for delivery, and practiced it, you are finished with the hardest part of your job. However, all the work you have done will be wasted if you fail to deliver your speech effectively.

Your method of delivery may vary, depending on a number of variables such as the purpose of your speech, the subject, the occasion, and your audience. Most of the time you will want to deliver your speeches extemporaneously. This is usually the best and most effective method. However, in some instances you might be required to deal with so many facts and statistics that you will want to write your speech out completely and deliver it verbatim so as not to run the risk of forgetting anything. On the other hand, you might be one of those gifted few who have the kind of retention and acting ability needed for delivering an effective memorized speech. If you are lucky, you will not be required at some future date to deliver an impromptu speech on the spur of the moment with no preparation at all. In case that happens, however, a number of suggestions are offered in this chapter to help you manage more effectively in that difficult situation.

As I have indicated, there are four principal methods of delivery: (1) impromptu, (2) memorized, (3) manuscript, and (4) extemporaneous.

IMPROMPTU SPEECHES

An impromptu speech is one that is developed on the spur of the moment. It demands a great deal of the speaker since it seldom gives time for advanced thought or preparation. When delivering an impromptu speech, you have little, if any, time to analyze the subject, audience, or occasion. You must think on your feet to choose and organize your material. While this can impart spontaneity and directness to your delivery, it can also result in inappropriate statements, unexpressed thoughts, and repetitiveness. Consider your own experience. How many times have you looked back at a situation and thought, "Why didn't I say that?" or realized that you had put your foot in your mouth and said the wrong thing?

There are times, however, when it is necessary to deliver an impromptu speech. If that situation arises, consider the following advice: (1) keep your speech short and to the point; (2) try to use illustrations for supporting material (from personal experience if possible); (3) handle only one main point; and (4) make sure your central idea and purpose are absolutely clear to your audience. Experience in the planning, preparation, and delivery of extemporaneous speeches will provide further guidelines for greater effectiveness in impromptu situations.

MANUSCRIPT SPEECHES

A manuscript speech is one that is completely written out in advance. It is used in situations where the presentation must be very precise. You would probably choose a manuscript speech if you were reporting to a group on a convention that you attended as their delegate or explaining a complicated statistical procedure. While the manuscript speech offers security to speakers afraid that they will forget what they want to say or say it badly, it has a number of disadvantages: (1) it reduces eye contact with the audience; (2) reading a speech in a spontaneous and convincing manner takes skill and practice; and (3) the speaker has difficulty in changing the language or content of a manuscript speech to adapt to the mood or reaction of the audience.

Even though you may be willing to accept these disadvantages in return for the security of a manuscript speech, the best advice is to deliver a manuscript speech only when time does not permit you to prepare and practice an extemporaneous speech or when exact word order is crucial to the success of the presentation. To deliver a manuscript speech effectively, consider the following suggestions.

1. Type your manuscript speech in capital letters, triple spaced and underlined to insure easy reading. Type on only one side of the paper and number the pages.

2. Edit your speech by reading each sentence aloud. Avoid overly long or complex sentences. No matter how involved or technical your material, it must be communicated clearly.

3. Indicate places of emphasis and pauses.

4. Practice your manuscript by reading it aloud at least three or four times. Become familiar enough with it so that you can maintain adequate eye contact. When possible, tape or video tape your delivery. You should sound as though you are talking to people, not reading to them.

5. Use appropriate facial expression and body action to enliven your delivery.

MEMORIZED SPEECHES

A memorized speech is written out as a manuscript speech and then committed to memory. While it appears to offer the advantages of a manuscript speech along with total eye contact, it has a number of weaknesses: (1) it takes an inordinate amount of time to memorize a speech, particularly a long one; (2) it takes a skillful actor to deliver memorized material in a natural, spontaneous way; (3) the speaker who delivers a memorized speech runs the risk of forgetting; and (4) as with the manuscript speech, it is difficult to change a memorized speech to adapt to feedback from the audience. However, for the right person, the memorized speech can be an excellent method, especially for someone who plans to give the same speech a number of times.

There are times when it would be desirable to commit part of a speech to memory. You might want to memorize the first few lines of the introduction to your extemporaneous speech in order to start positively and with total eye contact. Memorizing particularly suitable words or phrases can often produce positive results. Actually, most effective speakers use a combination of different delivery methods.

EXTEMPORANEOUS SPEECHES

Like the manuscript and memorized speech, the extemporaneous speech is carefully prepared in advance. The difference is that the speaker does not deliver the speech in a predetermined word order. Effective extemporaneous speakers usually develop their speeches in a complete-sentence outline form as shown in chapter 6. They know what they are going to say in the introduction, body, and conclusion of the speech but decide on the wording of the speech at the moment of delivery. You might compare extemporaneous speech delivery with the telling of a funny story. Most people tell a funny story extemporaneously. They are aware of the important details of the story and know how the story is going to unfold, but they haven't memorized the word order. As long as they include those details necessary to make the humor clear, they can tailor the story for any occasion. The result is a relaxed, spontaneous style, which is the main advantage of extemporaneous delivery.

Extemporaneous speakers often use note cards or an outline to help them move smoothly from one idea to the next. However, these cover the main and supporting ideas of the speech rather than the words used to express them. The extemporaneous method offers the same directness and spontaneity as the impromptu method without the danger of your rambling off the point or repeating yourself unnecessarily. For most situations, it is the most effective method of delivery.

PLATFORM MANNER

The term *platform manner* relates to the fact that most speakers deliver their speeches on a stage or platform raised above their audience. Your platform manner includes all of your nonverbal communication to an audience—the way you walk up to and away from the platform, your facial expression, posture, gesture, and attire. An audience will begin evaluating you as soon as you come into their line of vision. If you want to make a good impression, walk up to the speaker's platform in a firm, energetic way. This will say to them, "I have some things to offer you that I think you will find rewarding." After you have reached the lectern, pause briefly and look out at those in your audience in a friendly and interested way. If a smile is in order, smile. The important thing is that your facial expression should be appropriate to your subject matter; it should set the mood for your speech.

Maintain good posture when addressing your audience. Stand up straight but not rigid, with your weight evenly distributed on both feet. Avoid the temptation to lean on or slouch over your lectern. Speakers who look too casual tend to receive an indifferent response.

There may be times when it will become necessary for you to move around in front of your audience, to close the distance between you and them in order to emphasize an important point, to walk to a chalkboard or map, to use a projector or phonograph, or to demonstrate a way of doing something. There is one simple rule to follow in regard to movement. Whatever movement you make in front of your audience is acceptable as long as it appears to be motivated. If you walk to a window for no apparent reason and make no reference to something on the outside, your audience will find it distracting. Pacing back and forth aimlessly will have the same effect. Like the speech itself, your movement must have purpose.

Facial expression is another characteristic of platform manner. The face is more expressive in communicating nonverbally than any other part of the body. Flashing eyes, a wrinkled brow, a grimace, or a smile provide important signals to your audience about how to interpret the meaning of what you say. If you are concentrating on what you want to say, your facial expression will more than likely reinforce your speech. When delivering your speech, before you begin talking look around at your audience with a friendly expression on your face. This is an excellent way of establishing rapport with them and making you both feel at ease.

The way you gesture has much to do with determining the effectiveness of your platform manner. In casual, relaxed conversation, we habitually employ a wide range of gestures. Gestures are of two types: emphatic and descriptive. We nod our heads, shrug our shoulders, or wave our hands to emphasize what we have to say or to describe something.

If when presenting your speech you find it difficult to use gestures effectively, wait until you feel motivated to use them. In order to be effective, gestures must occur instinctively and spontaneously. For this reason, as I pointed out earlier, it is unwise to practice a certain gesture for a specific spot in your speech. Planned gestures usually look awkward or stilted.

A good rule of thumb to use with gestures is this: the bigger the audience, the broader the gestures, so that those in the back can see them. Gestures can be very effective in the speaking situation. However, keep in mind that an awkward gesture is worse than no gesture at all.

What we wear has an effect on the way people perceive us. When delivering your speech the clothes you wear should suit the occasion. For a classroom speech wear what you would normally wear to class. For a more formal occasion dress accordingly. In all cases your clothes should be clean, pressed, and in good repair.

Finally, make sure that the conclusion of your speech is carefully prepared or even memorized so that you can finish with your eyes fixed on the audience. After a brief pause, leave the speaker's platform with the same air of confidence with which you approached it. Never indicate by facial expression or gesture that you were dissatisfied in any way with your performance. Let your audience be the judge of that.

EYE CONTACT

When you are speaking to an audience, look directly at them. Hunt for eyeballs that are friendly and will let you in. Talking to those who express acceptance and interest will make the job of speaking easier. It is best to move slowly from looking at an individual in one part of the audience to one in another; if your eyes dart rapidly from person to person the effect will be shifty or unnatural. While it isn't necessary to look at each individual in the audience, be sure that you look at friendly faces in various parts of your audience. Do not develop the habit of looking mostly to one side of the room or at those who are nearest to you.

Eye contact is important for a number of reasons. First, it is an aid in holding attention. We indicate our interest in others by looking them in the eye. An audience will respond attentively to a speaker who demonstrates interest in them.

Second, as indicated above, we communicate to our audience nonverbally as well as verbally. We say a great deal with our facial expression, particularly the eyes. Facial expression can aid in making meanings clear, giving emphasis, and expressing moods. Naturally, an audience will have difficulty seeing your facial expression if you are buried in your notes or staring at the ceiling.

Third, eye contact is thought of as an indication of honesty and straightforwardness. Your audience is more likely to perceive you as being open and aboveboard if you can look them directly in the eye.

The final reason for maintaining eye contact is to obtain feedback from the audience. Thus, by their facial expression, posture, and gestures, we can often tell whether our listeners are interested or bored, friendly or hostile, clear or confused.

VOICE

As speakers, we use different variations of voice to communicate exactly what we mean. Our listeners get messages not only from what we say but also from the way we say it. For example, you could probably ask the question, "What did you say?" in half a dozen different ways by varying your tone or emphasis on words and thus changing the meaning. Try it and see. If you want to be an effective speaker, you must use different variations of voice to help make what you say more interesting and meaningful. The different characteristics of voice that help express meaning and variety are volume, rate, pitch, and quality.

Volume

Public speaking requires more volume than ordinary conversation. Rightly or wrongly, listeners tend to judge a speaker's credibility and confidence on the basis of his or her volume or the lack of it. A speaker with little volume is often thought of as being hesitant or withdrawn, while one who uses more volume is seen as being both positive and confident. While that is not always true, there is another reason for using adequate volume: it takes too much effort to listen to a speaker whose voice is not loud enough to hear easily. That is not to say, however, that a person should speak loudly throughout the presentation. A softening of tone can provide variety and interest to a speech. Two other elements of voice related to volume are force and intensity. Force is usually associated with loudness, although you can use either it or intensity to provide emphasis to a whisper.

Rate

Rate refers to the speed at which you speak and is usually stated in terms of the number of words spoken per minute. A typical rate for speaking and reading aloud would be around 125 words per minute. Rate is dependent on two elements—pause and duration. Duration refers to the length of time it takes to say a particular word. If a person cuts words off short and allows little pause, the rate of speech will be rapid. Beginning speakers often speak and read aloud at too rapid a rate. Effective speaking requires changes in rate and the use of pause and duration. Besides adding variety to a person's delivery, rate change, the use of pause before and after important points, and sustaining important words are effective in providing emphasis.

Quality

Although some voices sound very much alike, each of us has a unique and distinctive vocal quality. In fact, because every person's voice is unique and distinctive electronic voice prints are considered as accurate as fingerprints for purposes of identification. Therefore, it is a mistake to try to model your voice after another person's. In order to speak effectively you should maintain adequate breath support, speak at a comfortable pitch level, and remain relaxed when speaking. Except in speeches of criticism or when you are indicating annoyance or the like, you will want to speak in a voice that is pleasant. A pleasant voice should be free from breathiness, harshness, huskiness, hoarseness, and nasality. If any of these conditions occur regularly in your speaking, you should consult a speech therapist.

Pitch

Pitch refers to the placement of a speaker's voice on a musical scale. Each person has a natural pitch level at which he or she can speak most comfortably. This level is called optimum pitch. It should be located approximately in the center of a person's singing range. In speech the movement of pitch either upward or downward is called inflection. Speaking somewhere near the center of your singing range will allow you to inflect upwardly and downwardly with ease.

An effective speaking style is characterized by a variety of both upward and downward inflections. In relaxed conversation these inflections come naturally and spontaneously. They are indicators of both emphasis and meaning. The best way to insure that your inflection will add meaning and interest to your delivery is to develop your material so that you will be anxious to communicate it to your audience.

Articulation

Articulation is the process of forming the consonant and vowel sounds of words. These sounds are molded into language by the five articulators: lips, teeth, tongue, hard palate, and soft palate. Improper articulation results in indistinct speech. If you articulate your words poorly, you will be difficult to understand.

Sometimes speakers are unaware that they have problems with articulation. We learn to speak by imitating the speech of those around us. Consequently, our speech habits resemble the speech habits of those we have imitated. If, for example, someone grew up in a household or neighborhood where the *d* sound was substituted for the *th* sound, that person would undoubtedly say *dis* for *this*, *doze* for *those*, and so on and perhaps not even be aware of it.

The three most common errors in articulation are running words together, substituting one sound for another, and omitting necessary sounds. For example, *did you* becomes *di ja*, *student* becomes *stoont*, *asked* becomes *ast*, and so on. This kind of careless articulation is distracting to an audience. In order to deliver your speech effectively, you must make sure that your articulation is precise.

One of the best ways to become aware of any articulation problems you might have is to record your voice with a tape recorder. Tape yourself not only while practicing your speech, but during ordinary conversation as well. Listen to your articulation carefully. What are your problems? Substituting sounds? Running words together? Omitting necessary sounds? Once you have determined your problems, you can begin working to correct them. Keep in mind though, it took you a long time to form your bad habits, so it will take time and effort to eliminate them. But rest assured, it will be time and effort well spent.

Pronunciation

While articulation is the process of forming the consonant and vowel sounds of words, pronunciation is much more complex. It involves articulating the correct consonant and vowel sounds of a word and accenting that word in a proper manner. Or put in simpler terms, pronunciation means saying a word the way it should be said. Owing to the makeup of the English language, that is not always an easy task. There are several characteristics of our language that make the task even harder.

First, sometimes a letter in a word is silent and should not be articulated, for instance, the *w* in *sword* and the *s* in *island*. Remember, you cannot always tell how to pronounce a word just by looking at it. When you are not sure you are saying a word correctly, consult a standard dictionary.

Second, there are an inordinate number of ways to pronounce the same vowel in our language. People who study English as a second language are often frustrated by the fact that the same vowel is often pronounced differently in different words. For example, consider the six pronunciations of the letter *o* for the following words: *do*, *no*, *dot*, *oar*, *woman*, and *women*. Even some words that are spelled alike can require different pronunciations depending on the form they take. For instance, the word *read* as in, "Read the same passage you read yesterday."

Third, correct pronunciation requires knowing how to accent words of more than one syllable. This is more difficult in some cases than in others. While the word *contact* is accented the same regardless of whether it is used as a noun, verb, adverb, or adjective, the similar word contract has the accent on the first syllable when used as a noun but on the second syllable when used as a verb. The word *rebel* is even more irregular. Not only does the accent change depending on whether the word is used as a noun or a verb but the vowel sounds change as well. Thus, the phonetic pronunciation is indicated as [reb′ l] for the noun and [ri bel′] for the verb.

Finally, there are regional differences in pronunciation in the United States, called dialects. The East, the South, and the Midwest have their own dialects, and even within each region there are distinctive dialects as for example, black English. Because the majority of people in this country speak in a midwestern dialect, standard American dictionaries record this pronunciation. This does not, however indicate that a midwestern dialect is superior to any other. Therefore, rather than trying to change your manner of speech, follow the best usage for your particular dialect.

EXERCISES

Speech Assignments

1. *The impromptu speech.* Deliver a one-to-two-minute impromptu speech as your instructor directs. You will either be assigned a subject or be allowed to choose one of two drawn from a hat.

Delivery: Keep your speech short and to the point. Make sure your purpose and central idea are clear to your audience.

Sample Topics

1. The perfect age
2. My favorite teacher
3. The ideal husband (wife)
4. What I like (hate) about my job
5. Why _____ should be legalized
6. How to bounce a meatball

2. *A speech of criticism.* Deliver a two-to-three-minute speech criticizing a person, policy, or organization. Express your views in a direct, to-the-point manner, emphasizing your annoyance with the language you choose.

Delivery: This is an expression of viewpoint. You are not attempting to persuade someone to agree with you. Communicate your annoyance with appropriate gesture, facial expression, and tone of voice.

Sample Topics

1. Star Wars is stupidity.
2. Abortion is murder.

Name_____ Section_____ Speech#_____ Date_____

SPEECH EVALUATION SHEET

Grade _____

	Poor -	1	2	3	4	- Excellent	COMMENTS
A. DELIVERY							
1. Platform Manner							
2. Eye Contact							
3. Enthusiasm							
4. Confidence							
B. VOICE							
1. Volume							
2. Articulation							
3. Variety							
4. Quality							
C. CONTENT							
1. Introduction							
2. Use of Supports							
3. Knowledge of Subject							
4. Audience Analysis							
5. Conclusion							
D. LANGUAGE							
1. Clear							
2. Interesting							
3. Appropriate							

Figure 8-1.

3. My cousin is an idiot.

4. Our prison system is cruel and inhuman.

5. Welfare is another word for stealing.

The speech-evaluation form shown in Figure 8-1 is designed for both student and instructor evaluation. It lists those characteristics of content and delivery that should be considered when evaluating a speaker.

chapter nine

INFORMING

We live in an increasingly complex age—one of new technology, endless research, and specialization. Each year more and more new information is added to the sum total of human knowledge in our world. It is estimated that by the year 2000 there wili be 1000 times more knowledge in the world than there was in 1900. It is obvious, then, how important it is for us to be able to send and receive informative communication accurately and effectively.

All too often we take informative communication for granted. We listen to weather forecasts, news stories, stock market updates, and traffic reports with only half an ear and then wonder why we didn't get things straight. We give vague instructions as to where and when we're going to meet someone or exactly how we'd like our hair done and then become irritated when things go wrong. The purpose of informative communication is to add to a listener's understanding. In order to achieve this goal a speaker must communicate information clearly and interestingly. This chapter will deal with the three methods for communicating information: (1) exposition, (2) description, and (3) narration, followed by specific techniques for making your speeches both clear and interesting.

EXPOSITION

The primary purpose of exposition is to inform. It is communication that explains a concept, process, idea, or belief. It can include demonstration, explanation, analysis, and definition.

Demonstration

In order to show someone how to perform a card trick, prepare a salad, carve a turkey, or read palms you will want to use the technique of demonstration. Demonstration speeches can either involve participation from the audience or be nonparticipative. In demonstrating the card trick, for example, you might ask one or two members of the audience to try the trick to show how easily it can be learned. When demonstrating palm reading, you might have members of your audience read the lines and marks on their own palms to identify their life lines, their character, and so on. When members of your audience are observers rather than participants in your demonstration, you must be careful to present your material clearly and interestingly enough so that you achieve your purpose, audience understanding. Listed below are eight suggestions for making your demonstration speeches clear and interesting.

1. Practice your speech exactly as you plan to deliver it. If you are showing how to make a tossed salad, mix the ingredients in practice just as you

would in front of an audience. This will enable you to time your speech accurately. (It might take you longer to prepare and toss the ingredients than you thought it would.)

2. Determine whether the audience will see the usefulness of your demonstration. If it is not obvious to your audience that they have something to gain from paying attention to your demonstration, tell why your information will be useful to them during your introduction.

3. Break your speech down into units or steps so that it can be more easily followed by your audience.

4. Preview the steps you are going to follow in your introduction and summarize them in your conclusion. If your demonstration is long or complicated, consider a review of what has been said during the body of your speech.

5. Provide continuity to your discussion by talking throughout. Don't be like one young student who began her speech by saying, "Today I'm going to show you how to make Swedish meatballs," and then proceed to make them without saying another word for the next three minutes. Her meatballs were excellent; her speech was not.

6. Make sure that what you are showing the audience can easily be seen by all. Keep in mind that you must reach the entire audience, not just those in front. If you are not sure your demonstration can easily be seen, estimate the distance from your farthest listener and have a friend take a similar position to check visibility.

7. Maintain your cool. If you make a mistake, acknowledge it and go on. Your audience will appreciate the fact that you admitted your error.

8. Conform to a predetermined time limit for your speech. Before your speech you decided what you wanted to show your audience and how much time you wanted to spend doing it. Don't change that during your delivery.

Explanation

A second form of exposition is the explanation. The primary purpose of explanation is to make things clear or understandable. As a student, you are constantly involved with explanations. The school bulletin explains what courses your school offers and which ones you have to take to satisfy the requirements for your degree. Your instructors and advisors are primarily explainers. The syllabi you get at the beginning of the semester are explanations of what you will be studying in each course and what you are expected to accomplish.

The first rule to follow when you are going to use explanation is that you must thoroughly understand something before you can explain it to someone else. A second rule is always to use words in your explanation that will be clear to your audience. To use technical terms to explain a process or concept with which your audience is unfamiliar will be self-defeating. Note how Malcolm X uses references common to the experiences of his audience to explain what revolution is and is not:

> This is a real revolution. Revolution is always based on land. Revolution is never based on begging someone for an integrated cup of coffee. Revolutions are never based upon love-your-enemy and pray-for-those-who-spitefully-use-you. And revolutions are never waged singing "We shall Overcome." Revolutions are based upon bloodshed. Revolutions are never compromising. Revolutions are never based upon any kind of tokenism whatsoever. Revolutions overturn systems. And there is no system which has proven itself more corrupt, more criminal, than this system that in 1964 still colonizes 22 million African-Americans, still enslaves 22 million Afro-Americans.

> Source: Quoted in George Breitman, ed., *Malcolm X Speaks,* p. 50; copyright © 1965 by Merit Publishers and Betty Shabazz. Reprinted by permission of Pathfinder Press.

Analysis

Analysis involves breaking down a situation or concept into its parts in order to examine each part separately. It often asks such questions as, Who? What? Why? When? Where? How? It is used frequently in speeches to inform. When organizing a speech titled "How Our Government Operates," you might divide your speech into three parts: (1) the legislative, (2) the executive, and (3) the judicial, and examine each branch separately.

Explication is a form of analysis that makes clear what is obscure or implied. Often in this form of analysis you will want to use the testimony of experts to back up the information you are giving your listeners. Thus, in a speech titled "The Fallout Dangers of Star Wars," a student speaker quotes a noted authority to back up her thesis that "radioactive fallout from the proposed Star Wars system would probably devastate our environment and the entire human race":

> According to Dr. E. J. Sternglass, professor emeritus of radiological physics at the University of Pittsburgh School of Medicine, "A technologically perfect missile shield that is capable of intercepting every incoming nuclear warhead would in all probability still fail to protect the U.S. No shield, no matter how effective, would prevent radioactive fall-

out produced in space from damaging all living things on our planet. Not only would bombs exploded in space drop radioactivity on earth—but the defense system itself could add to the fallout.''

Source: With permission of the speaker, Melissa Gilchrist.

Evaluation is a third form of analysis. Perhaps, as a student, you have already been asked to give an end-of-the-course evaluation, or in the future you will have to evaluate a teacher, or the school, or yourself. When you use this technique, keep in mind that in order to be informative, evaluations must be objective. That is not always easy.

Reviews are a form of evaluation. Many of us listen to reviews on the radio or TV to decide which movies or programs we will watch or at which restaurants we will dine. Following is a student newspaper review of the album, *Raised on Radio,* by the rock group Journey:

Journey Delivers an Honest Effort—Finally!

If there was any band that I truly felt, after cutting a song in the studio, would sit back, smile, and giggle, ''Yeah, there's another million dollars,'' it would be Journey.

Believe it, folks, they were in it for the money. But somewhere between two members' departure and lead vocalist Steven Perry's successful solo L.P., the band got musically hungry.

The result, *Raised on Radio* (Columbia), is a fresh turning point for the band. Remember, though, we're talking about Journey, not the Talking Heads. You've got to expect some commerciality.

This time it's done in an honest, straightforward manner. The band is no longer hiding behind Perry's screeching vocals or Neil Schon's never-ending gutless guitar solos.

Sometimes the less you get the more you receive, and that's what makes the difference this time out. Utilizing different session bassists and drummers, original members Perry, Schon, and Jonathan Cain on Keyboards give each track a spirit all its own.

If you've ever felt tempted to buy an album by Journey but didn't because of its artificiality, try *Raised on Radio.* It's an honest effort by a band which, in the past, never cared about integrity.

Source: By Duane Rodriguez. With permission of the *MATC Times.* From the June 3, 1986, issue of the *Times.*

Definition

The primary purpose of informative communication is to be understood. This is unlikely to happen if you use language which is abstract or with which your audience is unfamiliar. When you must use abstract or unfamiliar words or concepts in your speech, define them so that your audience will know exactly what you mean. Your definitions can be either short or long and stated in your own words or the words of someone else. Avoid using dictionary definitions or ones that are overly complicated. Remember, your goal is to be understood. Following are specific suggestions for making your definitions clear to your listeners:

1. Define by example   This type of definition involves using detailed or undetailed examples to clarify a word or concept. It is especially useful when dealing with the abstract. For example, the word *love* is decidedly abstract. It has a different meaning for almost everyone. Therefore, if you use it in a speech, you will want to be sure that your listeners have a clear understanding of exactly what you mean when you used the term.

In a sermon delivered at the Dexter Avenue Baptist Church in Montgomery, Alabama, on Christmas 1957, the Reverend Martin Luther King, Jr., used the following examples to make clear to his audience exactly what he meant when he spoke of love:

> The meaning of love is not to be confused with some sentimental outpouring. Love is something much deeper than sentimental bosh. Perhaps the Greek language can clear our confusion at this point. In the Greek New Testament are three words for love. The word *eros* is a sort of aesthetic or romantic love. In the Platonic dialogues *eros* is a yearning of the soul for the realm of the divine. The second word is *philia,* a reciprocal love and the intimate affection and friendship between friends. We love those whom we like, and we love because we are loved. The third word is *agape*, understanding and creative, redemptive goodwill for all men. An overflowing love which seeks nothing in return, *agape* is the love of God operating in the human heart. At this level, we love men not because we like them, nor because their ways appeal to us, nor even because they possess some type of divine spark; we love every man because God loves him. At this level, we love the person who does an evil deed, although we hate the deed he does.

2. Define by comparison or contrast   An effective way of defining something unknown to your audience is by comparing it or contrasting it to something that is known. A fundamental principle of education is that the only way you can teach anything to students is to relate it to what they already know. Comparing the ideas that you are presenting to concepts that your listeners can relate to from their own experiences will improve your chances of success. In the following excerpt the author gives his reader a clearer understanding of the writing process by comparing it to building a wall:

In northern New England, where I live, stone walls mark boundaries, border meadows, and march through the woods that grew up around them long ago. Flank-high, the walls are made of granite rocks stripped from fields when pastures were cleared and used to fence in cattle. These are dry walls made without mortar, and the stones in them, all shapes and sizes, are fitted to one another with such care that a wall, built a hundred years ago, still runs as straight and solid as it did when people cleared the land.

Writing is much like wall-building. The writer fits together separate chunks of meaning to make an understandable statement. Like the Old Yankee wall-builders, anyone who wants to write well must learn some basic skills, one at a time, to build soundly.

Source: Roger Garrison, *How a Writer Works* (New York: Harper & Row, Publishers, 1981) p. 4.

3. Define by etymology   As you know, one of the reasons that English is such a difficult language to communicate with is that many of the words we use originated in other countries. Etymology refers to how and where a word originated and how it relates to other words in the English language. Sometimes a word can be better understood if you explain its "root" to your audience. For example, the word *genocide,* which originated during World War II as a result of the Nazis' attempt to exterminate the Jews, comes from the Greek *genus,* meaning "race," and the French *cide,* meaning "killing."

4. Define by details   Another method for defining terms that are abstract or complex is to discuss them in detail. Sometimes when you examine the parts of a picture, you get a better understanding of it as a whole. In the following example the author provides her audience with details to give them a clear understanding of how difficult survival is for children and senior citizens of the Ilk Tribe in the African country Uganda:

The Ilks turn their children out of the house when they are about three years of age. Parents make their children sleep in the open, providing their own shelter. The younger children of the tribe band together for protection against both the elements and older children. Even when the children fight viciously among themselves, the adults do not interfere. As a result, only the strongest children survive to take their places in adult society. This harsh treatment has purpose, because the Ilk consider children to be useless, expendable burdens, just as they do the aged. Adults are as cruel and neglectful of their elders as they are of their young children. Ilk elders who become sick and infirm are not fed or nurtured, but are simply allowed to fend for themselves or die.

Source: Grace J. Craig, *Human Development*, 2nd ed. (Englewood Cliffs, N.J.: Prentice-Hall, 1980) pp. 10–11.

5. Define with sensory aids   Can you imagine trying to explain the difference between country rock and acid rock without having your audience listen to an example of each? Try to describe orally the sound of a flute or synthesizer or the cry of a loon. Consider explaining the colors puce or magenta. The dictionary defines puce as brownish purple and magenta as purplish red. Does that give you a clear picture? Probably not. Have you ever prepared a meal of liver and onions? What does the liver feel like as your are cutting it? What does it small like when it is frying? What does it taste like when you eat it?

In some cases an oral explanation might be largely meaningless unless you have your audience also sensually experience the concept your are explaining. When delivering a demonstration speech which will be enhanced by the use of a sensory aid, use one. For example, if you are going to show your audience how to make brownies, bake a batch the night before and pass them out so they can taste the finished product.

DESCRIPTION

A second method of communicating information, description, makes use of sensory appeals to give the listener a clear picture of what is being communicated. You might give your listeners information about an object's appearance, what it sounds like, what it tastes like, and so on. The key to effective description is accurate, specific detail. The more accurate and specific your details are, the more likely it will be that your listeners will be able to get a clear picture of what you are describing. Note how in the following excerpt the writer uses specific detail to give his audience a clear picture of the city of Las Vegas:

> It's a 24-hour figment of some surreal imagination, a jerry-built collection of neon rising out of the red desert sand.
>
> Covered with sagebrush and tumbleweed, and decorated with several billion dollars' worth of glass, plastic, steel and concrete—Las Vegas transcends the normal definitions of reality.
>
> It is a town of high heels and sneakers, designer jeans and Levi's, gold neck chains and pale-green polyester leisure suits.
>
> It's a town where absolute strangers can meet at a bubbling fountain of free champagne, exchange life histories while filling their glasses, and depart, each knowing that neither will have to prove the truth of anything said to the other.
>
> They treat $100 bills like matchsticks here, but you can still make a public telephone call for a dime. Thirty-year-old blackjack dealers here have 50-year-old eyes. And 70-year-old hands.
>
> You can get a bacon, egg, toast and hashbrown breakfast at dinnertime for 99 cents, or a New York strip steak breakfast for $2.95. And you can catch a glimpse of Sinatra at Caesar's Palace, after a 2-hour wait, for $40—cocktails at $3.50 each, extra.
>
> This is a city of 6-foot showgirls not counting the feathers, of lavish and elaborate musical stage productions, of real celebrities doing real things like waiting for elevators.
>
> It is a town of 24-hour wedding chapels where there is no waiting period, and no blood test required; where marriage license may be obtained any time between 8 a.m. Friday and midnight Sunday, and between 8 a.m. and midnight any other day; and where almost 58,000 people were married last year, and where 9,000 were divorced.
>
> It is a city where a blissful couple, heedless of the 40-degree midnight temperature, can be found in their bathing suits sipping cocktails and dangling their legs in the heated waters of the hotel's outdoor swimming pool.

Source: Donald A Bluhm, *Milwaukee Journal*, March 20, 1983. Reprinted by permission.

NARRATION

Narration, the third model of communicating information, is sometimes called the story-telling method. Although narration is used most often to entertain or persuade, it can be a clear and interesting way to present information. Biographies and autobiographies are written to give us information about a person's life. When grandmother or grandfather tell you what life was like when they were your age, they are using narration to inform. An excellent example of a story to inform is the parable of the Good Samaritan, found in the tenth chapter of Luke in the Bible. In response to the question, "Who is my neighbor?" Jesus replies:

> A certain man was going down from Jerusalem to Jericho when robbers attacked him, stripped him and beat him up leaving him half dead. It so happened that a priest was going down the road; when he saw the man he walked on by, on the other side. In the same way a Levite also came there, went over and looked at the man, and then walked on by, but a certain Samaritan who was traveling that way looked upon him, and when he saw the man his heart was filled with pity. He walked over to him, poured oil and wine on his wounds and bandaged them; then he put the man on his own animal and took him to an inn where he took care of him. The next day he took out two silver coins and gave them to the innkeeper. "Take care of him," he told the innkeeper, "and when I come back this way again, I will pay you back whatever you spend on him." And Jesus concluded, which one of these three seems to you to have been a neighbor to the man attacked by the robbers?

> Source: From *Today's English Version of the New Testament.* Copyright © American Bible Society, 1966, 1971.

MAKE YOUR MATERIAL CLEAR

The purpose of informative speaking is to add to a listener's understanding. In order to do this a speaker must communicate clearly. You can help make your material clear by using words that are familiar and specific and by using descriptive gestures.

Use Familiar Words

Be assured, unless your listener understands the message, communication will not take place. Sometimes speakers are so concerned with impressing their audience with their vocabularies that they actually fail to communicate. This can be a serious mistake. Unlike the reader who can reread a passage that is unclear or look up words that are unfamiliar, the listener misses part of the message unless the words that the speaker uses are understood instantly. Therefore, when you choose your words as a speaker, always choose those that are the most familiar. For example, why say *fecund* instead of *fertile, efficacious* rather than *effective*, and so on? If you want everyone in your audience to understand you, use terms that are familiar to them. For example, in an 1866 speech to a group of English workingmen, Thomas Huxley, a renowned biologist, explained the process of induction in terms that were familiar to those in his audience. Here is an updated paraphrase of the speech Huxley delivered over 120 years ago:

> Suppose you go into a fruit shop wanting an apple—you take one up and upon biting it you find that it is sour. You look at it and see that it is hard and green. You take another one and that too is hard, green, and sour. The shopkeeper offers you a third, but before biting it you examine it and find that it is hard and green, and you immediately say that you don't want it since it must be sour like those you have already tried.
>
> Nothing can be more simple than that, you think; but if you will take the trouble to analyze and trace out into its logical elements what has been done by the mind, you will be greatly surprised. In the first place, you will have performed the process of induction. You found that in two experiences, hardness and greenness in apples went together with sourness. You found a general law, that all hard and green apples are sour; and that, as far as it goes, is a perfect induction.

In situations, however, where you must use words that are unfamiliar to your audience be sure to define the words before using them. This is especially important when using technical terms that you will be repeating over and over in your speech. There is no reason to avoid using an unfamiliar technical term. Just explain the term the moment you use it.

Use Specific Words

An effective way of making your ideas clear to others is to use specific language. To say that a person entered the room gives your listener little information. To say that he or she strutted, ambled, staggered, crept, or marched, says it more clearly. The word *tree* is general. *Fruit tree* is more specific. But *Bartlett pear, Courtland apple*, and *Bing cherry* are much more specific and therefore much clearer.

Sometimes a difficult concept can be made clear by explaining it in specific terms. Many people, for example, are unaware of the danger involved in improper disposal of nuclear waste. The student who began her speech, "Even though the dosages would be microscopic so that you couldn't even see them, if two pounds of plutonium could be evenly distributed among the world's population, each person on earth would receive a lethal dosage," used the specific to give her audience a better understanding as to the magnitude of the problem. The following excerpt from a TV speech delivered by President John F. Kennedy on October 22, 1962, uses specific language to explain exactly what was happening and to indicate particular cities that were threatened by the Cuban missile sites:

> This government as promised has maintained the closest surveillance of the Soviet military build-up on the island of Cuba. Within the past week unmistakable evidence has established the fact that a series of offensive missile sites is now in preparation on that imprisoned island. The purpose of these bases can be none other than to provide a nuclear strike capability against the Western Hemisphere.
>
> The characteristics of these new missile sites indicate two distinct types of installations. Several of them include medium-range ballistic missiles capable of carrying a nuclear warhead for a distance of more than 1,000 nautical miles. Each of these missiles, in short, is capable of striking Washington, D.C., the Panama Canal, Cape Canaveral, Mexico City, or any other city in the southeastern part of the United States, in Central America, or in the Caribbean area.
>
> Additional sites not yet completed appear to be designed for intermediate-range missiles capable of traveling more than twice as far, and thus capable of striking most of the major cities in the Western Hemisphere. This urgent transformation of Cuba into an important strategic base by the presence of these large long-range and clearly offensive weapons of sudden mass destruction constitutes an explicit threat to the peace and security of all the Americas.

Source: *Vital Speeches* 26 (November 15, 1962), 66.

Use Descriptive Gestures

Descriptive gestures aid by giving your audience a clearer picture of something. You might gesture to show your audience a proper golf swing or to give them an idea of the size of the tomatoes you grew. Or you might give your audience a clear picture of how effective karate can be for self-defense by demonstrating different karate techniques with a volunteer. Descriptive gestures not only make your ideas clearer, they also aid in maintaining audience interest.

MAKE YOUR MATERIAL INTERESTING

You must have the attention of your listeners if you want to communicate anything to them. You can help to hold their attention by making your material as interesting as you can. Two techniques that will help to achieve this goal in your communication are emphasis and variety.

Emphasis

We emphasize our ideas in speech nonverbally and with the words we choose. An upward inflection and an increase in volume often indicate great enthusiasm. You can tell when people are concerned by the intensity with which they say things. Tone of voice can emphasize. So can pause. Used before an important idea, pause says to an audience, "Pay close attention to what is coming next." A pause after an idea sets the idea apart and gives each listener a chance to reflect on what was said.

Besides being descriptive, gestures also emphasize. A positive movement of the hands or arms or a nod of the head may emphasize an idea or a point you are making. Leaning or moving toward your audience suggests interest or emphasis. Remember, gestures must be seen to be effective. A good rule of thumb is the larger the audience, the broader the gesture.

Another way to emphasize your ideas is to preview and summarize them. List the points you are going to make or steps you are going to follow in your introduction and summarize them in your conclusion. Or as one wag put it, "First, you tell them what you're going to tell them. Then, you tell them. And finally you tell them what you told them."

Variety

Most of us prefer to listen to a speaker with a pleasant, conversational style, one who seems to talk with you rather than to you. The key to the conversational style is speaking in a natural manner. In everyday conversation people speak with various vocal patterns to indicate the meanings they wish to convey. Their voices rise and fall as they inflect from one pitch to another, their volume increases or decreases depending upon their subject and how they feel about it, and their rate varies anywhere from 90 words a minute to over 180.

However, put many of these same people in a public-speaking situation and they become overly aware that some are forming opinions about what they say and the way they are saying it. They become conscious of how they look and sound and what they are saying. The result is that they lose their naturalness and spontaneity. They convey words (rather than meaning) in a flat, colorless way.

The next time you are engaged in enthusiastic conversation with your friends, make note of their speech patterns, gestures, and facial expressions. Yours will be similar. If you can transfer your animation and physical expression in informal conversation to public speaking, you will be more interesting and enjoyable to listen to and watch.

TYPES OF INFORMATIVE SPEECHES

As already indicated, the three methods for communicating information are exposition, description, and narration. Although the vast majority of speeches will contain a combination of these elements, most informative speeches can be listed in one of these three categories.

EXPOSITORY SPEECHES

Expository speeches explain a process, concept, idea, or belief. They include speeches to demonstrate, to explain a process, to instruct, and to review.

Speeches to Demonstrate

The informative-demonstration speech is designed to show your audience how to do something so that they will be able to do it on their own or have a better understanding of how it is done. Thus, you might deliver a demonstration speech to teach your audience how to make Swedish pancakes or to show them how various mathematical problems can be solved with a slide rule. As with most speeches, the key to delivering a demonstration speech successfully is effective audience analysis. You must ask the question, "What response can I reasonably expect from my listeners?" You could teach an audience to make Swedish pancakes in a reasonable amount of time; however, unless those in your audience were familiar with a slide rule, it seems unlikely that you could do much more than give them an understanding of how a slide rule can be used. Following are examples of demonstration speeches:

DEMONSTRATIONS TO TEACH	DEMONSTRATIONS FOR UNDERSTANDING
How to:	How:
wrap a gift	a parachute is packed
recognize cuts of beef	a head is shrunk
apply a tourniquet	belly dancing is done

DEMONSTRATIONS TO TEACH	DEMONSTRATIONS FOR UNDERSTANDING
How to:	How:
remove a stain	a lute is played
cover a book	a person is hypnotized
give a facial	fires get started
take good snapshots	an abacus is used
toss a salad	ballet is danced

Speeches to Explain a Process

Speeches to explain a process inform an audience how something works. While they are often organized similarly to demonstration speeches, they differ in purpose. A student studying photography might deliver a demonstration speech on how to take an effective snapshot. If he or she is asked to deliver an explain-a-process speech, an appropriate choice would be: how a camera works. Following are examples of explain-a-process speeches.

How:

a generator works	a microlaser operates
food is digested	a steam engine works
photosynthesis occurs	Project Elf functions
the eye functions	kidneys clean your blood

Speeches to Instruct

Instructive speeches are presentations in which the speaker gives facts and information about concepts or ideas. The topic of typical instructive speech would be: what makes the sky blue? These speeches can be thought of as informal class lectures. In order to deliver an instructive speech effectively, you should try to choose a subject that will be either useful or interesting to your listeners. Following are samples of instructive speeches:

Ideas of Thoreau	Solar energy
The chromatic scale	What controls the tide?
Nuclear submarines	Supply-side economics

Book Reviews

Reviews of current novels, television shows, short stories or plays can provide effective material for an informative speech. Choose one that you feel you are qualified to analyze and that will be interesting to your listeners.

DESCRIPTIVE SPEECHES

Descriptions of people, places, and events are part of our everyday communication. We insist on an in-depth description of our room-mate's cousin before agreeing to a blind date. We talk to a number of people who have vacationed at that new island paradise before we agree to go. We listen to a description of the events that took place at last year's homecoming game before buying our tickets for this year's game. Following are four types of descriptive speeches:

Introducing Yourself

Perhaps one of the first speeches you will be asked to deliver is one in which you introduce yourself to the rest of the class. Since you should be an authority on yourself, the content of this speech should pose no problem for you. Include those things that you feel will be of interest to the class.

Introducing a Classmate

Another type of introductory speech involves describing a classmate to your audience. Describe his or her accomplishments, talents, hobbies, goals, likes and dislikes, or anything you think will be of interest to the class.

Describing a Place

A vivid description of your home town or favorite place can make an effective speech. This can be a particularly effective presentation when the speaker is describing a location with which most of the audience is unfamiliar.

Describing an Event

The description of an event can be an effective informatory speech. An eye-witness account of the Olympic games, a rocket launching, a bank robbery, or other such topics could be developed into exciting, attention-holding presentations.

NARRATIVE SPEECHES

Narration or storytelling may be employed in speeches to entertain, persuade, or to inform. Although not everyone can tell one well, everybody loves a funny story. Many anecdotes, fables, and parables have persuasion as their primary purpose. If you simply tell a friend what happened to you on a particular day, your purpose is to inform.

A Personal Experience to Inform

Personal experience speeches arc easy to develop, particularly if the incident you are relating actually happened to you. One type of informative speech is relating to your audience a personal experience which helped you to mold your image of yourself. In this speech, your job is to develop your story so that your audience is able to perceive your reaction to the situation and to understand how that reaction gave you a clearer picture of yourself.

A Historical Narrative

The historical narrative speech involves telling a story about an episode or sequence of events in history. A vivid description of the scene, characters, and setting of the battle of the Alamo would effectively hold an audience's attention. Following are samples of historical narratives:

The Battle of Bunker Hill	Custer's last stand
The rise of Hitler	The Valentine's Day massacre
The Great Society	My Lai

SAMPLE PERSONAL-EXPERIENCE-TO-INFORM SPEECH

The following classroom speech was presented in a public speaking class for business people at the University of Wisconsin Extension. It provides a clear model for the informative speech of personal experience.

TOUGH BUT STUBBORN

I discovered even before I started school that I was a tough kid. We lived in a downstairs flat on the east side, next to a bakery. Across the street was a Catholic church and grade school. In the spring during recess, the boys would play baseball on the school grounds. Often, I would walk across the street and watch while they were choosing sides, hoping someone would pick me, but no one ever did. I guess it was because I was too small; I had just turned five years old. One day, after I had been passed over by these boys, I got mad and grabbed their ball. I told them that I would not give it back unless they let me play. A kid with a bat ran up to me and hit me over the head with it. It really hurt but I gritted my teeth and fought back the tears. Angrily, I threw the ball onto the school roof and stalked home.

As I walked up the front stairs, my mother, who had spotted me through the front window, rushed to the door. "Good Lord, what happened?" she screamed.

"Some guy hit me with a bat," I said casually.

She quickly pulled me into the bathroom and as she was wetting a washrag, I looked into the mirror. I saw then why she had sounded so frightened. My blond head was bright red from blood, which had begun to run down my face and ears. My mother cleaned me and said she hoped I had learned my lesson, but the next day there I was, as usual, standing next to the boys on the playground, waiting to get chosen. This time, however, I had a huge white bandage on my head.

SAMPLE UNDETAILED OUTLINE FOR SPEECH TO INSTRUCT

In the instructive speech, the speaker gives facts or information about a concept or idea. The following undetailed outline together with a complete introduction and conclusion provides a clear model for this type of speech.

BLACK AND BEAUTIFUL

Introduction

Did you know that the first doctor to perform open heart surgery, Dr. Daniel Hale Williams, was black? Or that Chicago was founded by a black pioneer named Jean Baptiste Dusable? Or that Mathew Hensen, another black man, was with Robert Perry when he discovered the North Pole? I learned these and many other interesting facts when I attended a series of campus-lectures on the accomplishments of blacks during Black History Week last year. Today, I'm going to share some of that information with you. I'm going to talk about how blacks have helped both to develop this nation and to defend it; about the contributions of blacks in medicine, art, music, and literature; about black contributions in the areas of politics and religion, and of the long and impressive list of black leaders in the areas of sports and entertainment. The list is long and impressive and I hope that by the time that I have concluded, you will have a better understanding as to how much black Americans have helped this nation during the last two hundred plus years.

   I.   Throughout our history, black men and women have contributed significantly to the growth and improvement of the United States.
       A.   Blacks have helped both to develop this nation and to defend it.
       B.   Blacks have served illustriously in the field of medicine.

    C. Black contributions to art, music, and literature have been impressive.

II. Today's black leaders have done much to improve government and the quality of life in our country.

    A. Black public officials have become a viable force on the political scene.

    B. Black religious and moral leaders have acted as the conscience of America.

    C. The list of black leaders in the field of sports and entertainment is long and impressive.

Conclusion

This nation therefore owes a debt of gratitude to black Americans. Blacks have helped to develop this country and to defend it. They have made significant inroads in the field of medicine. Blacks have made impressive contributions in the fine arts. Many black actors, musicians, writers, and artists are world renowned. Other blacks have shaken the conscience of America through their moral and religious leadership. Blacks have long been a viable force on the political scene and the list of blacks in sports and entertainment is seemingly endless. It is easy to see why many feel that the words ''black'' and ''beautiful'' are synonymous.

EXERCISES

Speaking Assignments

1. *Demonstration speech.* Deliver a three-to-five-minute speech in which you demonstrate a technique or procedure. Pick something you enjoy doing and do well. Consider whether your audience will see the usefulness of your information. Topics that offer little utility to an audience must be made interesting to hold attention.

Delivery: This speech should be delivered extemporaneously. Demonstration speeches require freedom of movement. Practice this speech thoroughly so that you can deliver it easily and naturally. The less dependent on your outline or notes you are, the better.

SAMPLE TOPICS

1. How to remove spots inexpensively.
2. How to toss a salad.
3. How to wrap a turban.

4. How to make a Greek salad.
5. How to perform a magic trick.

2. *Speech to instruct with visual aid.* Prepare a four-to-six-minute speech to instruct using a visual aid. Choose a subject that you find interesting and whose effectiveness will be increased by the use of a visual aid. Organize your speech carefully, choosing visual aids that will effectively add to the listeners' understanding.

Delivery: This speech should be delivered extemporaneously. You must be able to move around freely when using an aid. Refer to chapter 4 for suggestions on how to use visual aids effectively.

SAMPLE TOPICS

1. The hemispheres of the brain.
2. The vampire bat.
3. The principle of radar.
4. Tax reform.
5. The vikings.

3. *Introducing a classmate.* Interview a classmate, questioning her about her hobbies, goals, attitudes, accomplishments, or anything you feel will be of interest to the class. Take careful notes. Then have your classmate interview you. Develop your presentation in an interesting way and put it in an order that will be easy for you and your audience to remember.

SUGGESTIONS

1. Pronounce your classmate's name distinctly and correctly.
2. Be as friendly and as enthusiastic as you can.
3. Be accurate. Check your facts before you deliver the speech.
4. Be familiar with your material. If you need notes use only one note card.

chapter ten

PERSUASION

When you think of the word *persuasion*, what mental picture occurs to you? Do you visualize a TV commercial done by some slick multimillion-dollar advertising agency? Do you picture a political candidate who would promise almost anything if it meant getting elected? Do you envision someone selling condos, used cars, or magazines? Do you see yourself trying to get a few extra days to finish that term paper or pay off that loan? It might very well be that you see all of these images and more because in this country persuasion is so much a part of our society and our lives.

We are involved with persuasion daily both as receivers and senders. We are constantly being bombarded with appeals to "get with it," to "enjoy life," and to give ourselves "the very best." We spend a lot of our time talking to others trying to get them to act a certain way, to agree with our point of view, or just simply to like us more.

The two main differences between this one-to-one persuasion and delivering a persuasive speech are that the latter involves talking to more people and spending more time and effort in planning, preparation, and delivery. Otherwise, the methods are basically the same.

PERSUASION DEFINED

Persuasion can be defined as *a conscious attempt to influence the thought or behavior of others through the use of personal, psychological, and logical appeals.* Let us examine this definition in detail.

First, consider the word *conscious*. You must know that your purpose is to persuade. The more aware you are of exactly what you wish to accomplish, the more likely you are to be successful. An informative speech may also persuade, but if its primary purpose is to inform, then the persuasion is accidental.

The second word to remember is *attempt*. Whether you are successful or not, you are still involved in persuasion. The vacuum cleaner salesperson can make a good living delivering the same sales pitch to ten customers a day, even though only two or three of them buy the product.

The third important word is *influence*. You don't have to sell the product immediately to be a successful persuader. Persuasion can be a long-range process, which influences thought or behavior a little at a time. Consider, for example, an attempt to improve the image that minority residents of a major city have of the police department. You can't expect to change overnight attitudes that for some it took years to develop. The best you might be able to expect from some of these citizens is to make them a little less antagonistic toward the police.

Finally, there are three appeals or types of proof in the definition that persuaders use to sell their products more effectively: personal, psychological, and logical.

PERSONAL PROOF

Over two thousand years ago the Greek philosopher Aristotle stated that no other factor was more important to success in persuasion than the audience's perception of a persuader as having good sense, good moral character, and good will. Speech experts agree that this principle is as true today as it was then. No factor is more important to your success as a persuader than the image your listener has of you as a person. Ideally, you want your audience to see you as a competent person who has integrity and goodwill toward them. If they do, your chances of being successful as a persuader are excellent.

Competence

Competence means being well qualified, having good sense, knowing what you are talking about. Most of us are influenced by those who are capable. When we have problems with our electronic equipment, we take it to an expert to have it fixed. When our dentist tells us that we need a root canal, we set up an appointment. When our doctor tells us that our appendix must be removed immediately, we agree.

To be an effective persuader you must project an image of competence to your audience. To a great extent this will depend on how much time and effort you put into preparing and delivering your speech. A carefully organized, clearly worded speech is the mark of a competent communicator. Following are five specific suggestions you can use to project an image of competence to your audience:

1. Articulate your words clearly and use correct grammar and pronunciation. A listener is likely to question your ideas if they are unclear or expressed incorrectly.

2. Be up to date. A competent person uses the most current information available.

3. Indicate your qualifications. If you have education or experience that provides you with special knowledge about your subject, indicate this during your introduction.

4. Speak with confidence. One of the characteristics of the competent person is a positive approach.

5. Be fluent. Practice your speech so that you can deliver it easily and naturally. Whether justified or not, listeners often judge nonfluency as an indication of poor preparation or indecision.

Integrity

Have you ever had the feeling that a politician you were listening to was just a little too smooth, or that even though you couldn't put your finger on it, there was something that made you wonder if you could trust a particular salesperson? In today's world, with its hypocrisy and credibility gaps, integrity is of major concern to an audience. Before an audience will accept your ideas they must feel that you are worthy of their trust and respect. Following are specific suggestions that will help you indicate to your audience that you are sincere and honest:

1. Dress appropriately. Your chances of achieving a desired response will be greater if you dress according to the expectations of your audience.
2. Establish a common bond. Listeners are more inclined to respond positively to a speaker they see as having similar attitudes, values, and experiences.
3. Be objective. To be effective, you must show your audience that you are presenting your views fairly and fully.
4. Indicate your motives. If you have strong motives for presenting your viewpoint, indicate these to your audience. Even if they don't agree with you, they will admire your convictions.
5. Be sincere. You are more likely to project an image of sincerity if your tone of voice and facial expression are appropriate to what you are saying.

Goodwill

"The key to success for a salesman is to be well liked," says Willie Loman in Arthur Miller's play, *Death of a Salesman.* While this is an oversimplification, being well liked is an important qualification for a salesperson to have. People are much more likely to buy something from someone they like than from someone they are indifferent to or don't like. Therefore, one of the most important things you do as a persuader is to get your audience to like you. The best way to do this is to show that you like them. Here are some specific suggestions you can use to enhance your image as a person of goodwill:

1. Show enthusiasm. Greeting your audience in a lively energetic way will show them that you are interested in them and happy to be there.
2. Use tact. You can project an image of goodwill by being diplomatic and flexible, especially when dealing with an issue to which some of your listeners are opposed.

3. Be respectful. Treat your listeners with courtesy. Give them credit for having ability, uniqueness, and intelligence.
4. Use humor. An attitude of friendliness is projected by a speaker's use of humor. When used effectively, humor causes both the speaker and the audience to relax.
5. Establish rapport. *Rapport* is a French word meaning "to bring harmony." You can establish rapport with your audience by showing that you like them. Whenever you can, make reference to those in your audience. If you are on a first-name basis with some, refer to them whenever it suits the occasion.

IMAGE

In persuasion, the term *image* refers to a mental picture that a customer has of the product that the persuader is selling. That product can be political candidates, a company, a brand of wine, and so on. When you deliver a persuasive speech, the "product" you are selling is you. As you have seen, you want your listeners to have a mental picture of you as a person of competence, integrity, and goodwill. If they do, your personal proof will be strengthened, and the chances that they will believe you will be greater.

CREDIBILITY

There is a positive relationship between image and credibility: the better the image, the better the credibility. Conversely, a person with a poor image has low credibility. The strength of personal proof can clearly be demonstrated by examining the image-credibility relationship of Dr. Martin Luther King, Jr. As a highly educated, renowned speaker and writer, this national figure projected an image of competence. As a Baptist minister, civil-rights leader, and winner of the Nobel Peace Prize, he projected an image of integrity. And as a leader who was so close to his followers that he marched with them, slept with them, and went to jail with them, he projected an image of goodwill. Among his supporters King's credibility was so high that many of them risked harassment, jail, personal injury, and even their lives to follow him.

PSYCHOLOGICAL PROOF

The second appeal used by persuaders to sell their products is psychological proof. Psychological proof appeals to the attitudes and motives of the audience. We tend to act in certain ways because of two factors: attitude and motive.

Attitude often determines the way we are going to act, and motive supplies the impulse or desire to act.

Attitudes

Attitudes are learned. We form them from our education and experience and from our interaction with others. For example, we form favorable or unfavorable attitudes about government, religion, abortion, communism, sex, and so on. These attitudes give direction to our behavior causing us to act in predisposed ways in different situations.

Motives

The inner drive or impulse that stimulates behavior is called motive. If you consider attitude as the directive force of behavior, motive could be considered the driving force. There are two basic types of motives: physical motives and social motives.

Physical Motives   Often referred to as basic human drives, physical motives are common to people of all societies. All of us are born with the same basic physiological needs. We want to eat when hungry, drink when thirsty, defend ourselves when threatened, seek safety from the weather, and so on. For many of us in the United States, these basic needs are being abundantly satisfied. And the more money we have, the more we spend to achieve the greatest possible comfort. We buy central air conditioning, contour furniture, and heated swimming pools to pamper our most priceless possession, ourselves. We are, to a great extent, creatures of the body. Although it is unlikely that you will encounter a situation where your listeners have not satisfied their physical needs, making them aware of those who have not can often be quite effective.

Social Motives   A baby is born with a set of physical motives but without social motives. These are learned. No doubt the first social motive the infant develops is the security motive. This motive is primary to the newborn baby and continues as a powerful need at least until the child goes off to school. The tendency of little children to cuddle up; carry a doll, teddy bear, or security blanket around; or hide behind mother when a stranger comes to the door are all examples of the strength of this motive in the small child.

Another motive that develops during this period of closeness to the mother is the approval motion. The baby soon learns that cooing, smiling, laughing, and the like, win approval. The child also soon finds that while some things win a pat on the back, others result in a pat on the backside. Approval becomes an important need for the child. For some children the need for approval is so strong that isolation becomes a significant punishment. Banishing a child to his or her room with the comment, "Go to your room. I don't want to see you any more today,'' can be devastating for some. During this time, children also develop their own attitudes of approval or disapproval toward themselves.

Specific Motive Appeals

Sex. Perhaps no motive is appealed to more often in persuasion than the sex motive. Advertising in this country is supersaturated with sex to sell everything from shock absorbers to perfume. Records are sold with jacket covers featuring attractive women or handsome men who have absolutely no relationship to the music inside. Automobiles, cigarettes, toothpaste, and diet sodas are all used by young, vibrant, ''beautiful'' people, and if you use these products, somehow you will be beautiful too. Be assured, the sex motive plays an important role in all areas of persuasion.

Security. Another appeal often used in advertising is the security motive. The effect that this motive has on us and our loved ones is clearly evident in today's society. We have banks to protect our money, unions to protect our jobs, and insurance companies to provide for our health care, and when the time comes, for our survivors.

We go to college to provide for a more secure future, we ''go steady'' to insure a dependable date, and we put money aside for a ''rainy day.'' In this age of violence and uncertainty, no generation has been as security minded as this one.

Approval. Whether it be at home, at work, at school, or among friends, we are constantly seeking the approval of others. Any advertisement that features brand names is selling approval along with the product. A person might spend months landscaping a back yard or painting a picture for the satisfaction of being able to say, ''I made this myself.''

One effective technique in persuasion is to take the feeling of approval away from an individual, making the person feel uncomfortable. An example is the priest, rabbi, or minister making hell ''hot'' for the congregation. Another example is the ad that talks about the starving children of the world pointing out that the average dog in this country eats better than many children in the rest of the world or that the average American citizen throws away enough garbage per day to feed a family of six in India. The idea is that the readers or listeners feel uncomfortable about the situation until they contribute their money in an effort to help.

Conformity. Closely related to the approval motive is the motive to conform. Even in the most primitive societies, people have customs, mores, and rules to which they must conform in order to live in harmony with their peers. Most people tend to go along with the group rather than swim against the stream. Have you ever, for example, worn a style that was not particularly becoming to you because it was the thing to do? Or would you dare show up in jeans at a formal dance?

Early in life you learned to conform to the expectations of those around you. As you grew older and came in contact with more people, you found that conforming to these expectations becomes considerably more difficult. You could, for example, be labeled un-American for conforming to the expectations of a Christian "peace group" or un-Christian for advocating the nuclear destruction of Communist nations.

Success.   The desire to succeed can be a powerful motive. For some it is so intense that it overshadows all others. Individuals have been so strongly motivated to succeed that they have lied, cheated, and even killed to further this ambition. Advertisers have used the success motive to sell products ranging from toothpaste to condominiums. The success motive has long been used to sell luxury cars. People who buy Lincoln Continentals, Cadillacs, Corvettes, and Thunderbirds are buying success along with the automobile.

Creativity.   Creativity is one of the motives that can be unusually forceful. It is a form of self-actualization. Some have spent years of self-sacrifice and deprivation in an attempt to develop an artistic or musical ability. Who hasn't heard of a starving artist's sale or an author who could paper a room with rejected slips from publishers. The fact that these people continue creating testifies to the strength of this motive.

It should be pointed out that while a person may be more influenced by one motive than another at any given time, motives seldom operate individually. Sometimes two or more motives combine to affect a person's behavior. A person might be motivated to lift weights for a number of reasons. Weight lifting conditions the body, satisfying the good-health motive. It develops muscles and a trim figure, satisfying both approval and popularity motives.

At other times motives are in conflict with each other. Take, for example, the person who attends a party where drugs are being used. To refuse to go along with the group can threaten that person's popularity and peer approval, but to use the drugs can be a threat to security and parental approval. As you can see, motives have a significant impact on people's lives.

LOGICAL PROOF

Reasoning is the process of drawing conclusions from evidence. There are two kinds of evidence: evidence of fact and evidence of opinion. The explanation of this reasoning process to others in an attempt to influence belief is called argumentation. A basic argument consists of two statements: a premise and a conclusion drawn from that premise. Here are two basic arguments:

1. Mark is a member of the American Nazi party. Therefore, he is a troublemaker.
2. Mark has been arrested three times. Therefore, he is a troublemaker.

Both statements involve a premise-conclusion relationship. In the first example the conclusion is drawn from the fact that Mark is a member of the American Nazi party. "Mark is a member of the American Nazi party. Therefore, he is a troublemaker." This argument is based on deductive reasoning. You have come to the conclusion that Mark is a troublemaker because he belongs to the American Nazi party. You reason from a general premise (Members of the American Nazi party are troublemakers) to a minor premise (Mark is a member of the American Nazi party) to the conclusion (Therefore, Mark is a troublemaker). Whenever you reason from a general rule to a specific case, you are reasoning deductively.

The second statement, "Mark has been arrested three times. Therefore, he is a troublemaker," is an example of inductive reasoning. There is no rule to guide the reasoner, only the observation about Mark: he has been arrested three times. Therefore, he is a troublemaker. When you come to a conclusion as the result of observing or experiencing individual situations or cases, you are using inductive reasoning. Although you may not have been aware of it, this is a form of reasoning that you have used throughout your life. Do you like pizza? Enjoy rock music? Think that you are a good student? Whether your answer to these questions is yes or no, it has undoubtedly been based on inductive reasoning. You probably decided whether you liked pizza after eating one, three, five, or more. The same was true about your attitude toward rock music and your status as a student. Your observation or experience with these involvements has determined your conclusion.

DEDUCTIVE REASONING

As you can see, induction draws conclusions from specific experiences or observations, and deduction begins with the acceptance of a general rule (as stated in a major premise) and applies it to a specific case in the conclusion. In most cases deductive reasoning is stated in a form called an enthymeme, where one of the premises or sometimes the conclusion is not expressed but implied. This was the case with the deductive statement above: John is a member of the American Nazi party. Therefore, he is a troublemaker.

When formally stated, deduction is expressed in a three-step pattern called a syllogism. The reasoning moves from a major premise to a minor premise to a conclusion. In the example above the major premise was not expressed but implied. The formally stated syllogism would appear this way:

Major premise: Members of the American Nazi party are troublemakers.

Minor premise: Mark is a member of the American Nazi party.

Conclusion: Therefore, Mark is a troublemaker.

It is often useful to examine a syllogism by putting it in this formal, three-step form. This makes it easier to determine (1) whether the major and minor premises are true, and (2) whether the conclusion follows logically from them. A syllogism can be thought of as a framework for deductive logic.

Keep in mind that while inductive reasoning moves from specific instances to a general conclusion, deductive moves from a general rule (Heavy smokers are likely to get lung cancer) to a minor premise (Helga is a heavy smoker) to a specific conclusion (Therefore, Helga is likely to get lung cancer).

In order to use deductive reasoning effectively as a speaker, you must get your audience to agree with your major and minor premises and present a conclusion that follows logically from the premises. To do this, you will need to support your premises with evidence.

Suppose, for instance, that you are delivering a speech on the undesirability of eating too many meals at fast-food restaurants, and one of your points is that much of the food served in fast-food restaurants is extremely high in cholesterol. Your deductive argument would be expressed in a syllogism similar to this one:

Major premise: High-cholesterol foods are dangerous to your health.

Minor premise: The food served at fast-food restaurants is mostly high in cholesterol.

Conclusion: Therefore, the food served at fast-food restaurants is dangerous to your health.

Now that you have constructed the syllogism, you need to get your audience to agree with your premises. If they accept your premises as true, and if the premises are set up properly, then they will agree with your conclusion if it follows logically from the premises. First you will have to present evidence to get your audience to agree with your major premise: high-cholesterol foods are dangerous to your health. You might quote the testimony of one or two experts on the subject. Choose people your audience will consider objective and well qualified. You could quote recent statistics or research studies. Perhaps an explanation of the effects of cholesterol on the body would be effective.

When you have supported your major premise adequately, you are ready to deal with the minor premise: The food served at fast-food restaurants is mostly high in cholesterol. Certainly, you would give examples of the kinds of high-cholesterol foods you are talking about: hamburgers, french fries, and fish fried in animal fat, and the like. Following this you might use comparative statistics to show the contrast between these foods and the kinds you would eat in a well-balanced diet.

If you have succeeded in getting your listeners to agree with your premises, they will accept your conclusion: Therefore, the food served in fast-food restaurants is dangerous to your health. The test of a good conclusion must always be, Does it follow logically from the evidence that has been presented? If you have supplied your listeners with enough evidence to get them to accept your major and minor premises, they will accept your conclusion. When used correctly, deductive reasoning can be an effective form of persuasion.

INDUCTIVE REASONING

As you have seen, deductive reasoning moves essentially from a general rule to a specific conclusion. Inductive reasoning, on the other hand, reverses this process. When you reason inductively, you examine specific instances and as a result of your observations come to a general conclusion. For example, if you have had good service from three cars, a Pontiac, a Chevrolet, and a Buick, you might come to the conclusion that a General Motors product is a good car to own. If you have read statistics that show that people with college degrees earn far more than those who are less educated, then you might have concluded that college is the place for you. Both of these forms of reasoning are primarily inductive. The first, generalization, examines individual cases—three GM automobiles—and concludes that what is true about these specific cars is also true about GM products in general. The second, statistics, involves drawing conclusions from numerical evidence. If the figures show that people with college degrees earn more, then the chances are that if we get a higher education, we will make more money too. Let us look at these two forms of inductive reasoning in more detail.

Reasoning by Generalization

This type of reasoning involves examining specific details or examples and coming to a general conclusion. If there are a limited number of instances involved, the more you cite, the more probable the conclusions. For example, you might argue that Senator Jones is prolabor and Senator Smith antilabor by citing their voting records on legislation affecting labor.

When used well, generalization can be an effective argument in persuasion. Carefully controlled scientific experiments and studies can provide strong evidence for your speeches.

Reasoning by Statistics

This form of inductive argument involves drawing conclusions from numerical evidence. There are many who are suspicious of statistics. It has been said that one can prove anything with numbers. However, when used properly, statistics can provide a compelling argument. One example of statistics that work is the poll predicting the winner in an upcoming election. By taking a random sampling from a cross section of the voting population in a given area, pollsters can accurately predict the outcome of that election. Another example is the controlled test. Ten thousand people are tested to determine the effectiveness of a new vaccine. If the vaccine is effective for 98 percent of the test group, it will probably be effective for 98 percent of the total population. When used properly, statistics can be very persuasive. Here are a number of suggestions to follow when using statistics:

1. Document Statistics

When the statistics you are using are consistent with the general knowledge and experience of your audience, there is no need to indicate their exact source. However, when using statistics that are not widely known, indicate when and by whom the statistics were compiled.

2. Make Statistics Clear

Since it is quite likely that some in your audience have been deceived in the past by statistics, it is important that you explain statistics clearly whenever you use them.

3. Round Off Statistics

When dealing with large numbers, it is a good idea to round them off. Instead of saying that the population of Denmark is 4,952,000, round it off to an approximate 5 million.

4. Dramatize Statistics

If you can dramatize your statistics, they are more likely to be understood and remembered. For example, to say, "In Hong Kong, one person in fifty is an opium user, and a habit there costs about $650 a year to support," dramatizes the problem much more effectively than giving a statistical percentage.

OTHER FORMS OF REASONING

Reasoning by generalization and by statistics is primarily inductive. However, reasoning by comparison and by cause-and-effect mixes induction and deduction.

Reasoning by Comparison

Argument by comparison involves the examination of two similar cases. If the two have enough similarities, it is possible to argue that what is true of one case will be true of the others as well. The comparisons may be either literal of figurative. Literal comparisons compare things that are within the same categories, such as U.S. inflation rates in 1987 and 1988 and a comparison of academic standards at different universities. If the similarities in the literal comparisons are significant, the conclusions often appear logical.

Figurative comparisons point out similarities between things in different categories. Comparisons between life and a pathway and between the kingdom of heaven and a sower of seeds are examples of figurative comparisons. Although figurative comparisons are often weak as arguments since they are based on only one major similarity, they are both popular and colorful and also useful in relating the unknown to the known.

Reasoning from Cause and Effect

Causal reasoning is based on the principle that every cause has an effect. When two things occur together with any frequency, we might naturally determine that one is caused by the other. For example, the person who complains, ''Every time I eat pizza, I get heartburn,'' might logically assume that the pizza has triggered the heartburn. However, since cause-and-effect relationships can often be quite complicated, it could be that the heartburn is caused by a gall-bladder disorder, which was aggravated by eating the pizza, so that rather than giving up pizza, the person should see a doctor.

Causal relationships are most clearly demonstrated in carefully controlled situations. For example, a number of years ago researchers were interested in finding out what effect music had on the milk production of dairy cows. They used two experimental groups and a control group. Each group of cows was housed in the same-size barn, fed the same food, and matched in every relevant way, except that after the first week, light classical music was piped into barn A, hard rock into barn B, and no music into barn C. The results of the experiment, which ended after week 2, were that group A produced half again as much milk as they had during week 1, group B's production was reduced by one-third, and group C's production remained the same. The experiment showed clearly what effect the music had on the cows.

Keep in mind that causal relationships are more difficult to identify in less controlled situations. This is especially true in political, economic, and social situations, which frequently have multiple causes.

TYPES OF PERSUASIVE SPEECHES

Persuasive speeches can be classified into three types: (1) speeches to convince; (2) speeches to reinforce; and (3) speeches to actuate. Careful audience analysis is essential in persuasive speaking. The type of persuasion a speaker chooses should be based upon the attitudes of the audience prior to the speech and the specific changes sought.

Speeches to Convince

There are times when a persuader must deal with an audience that is either undecided, indifferent, or opposed to a proposition.

President Reagan defending his budget cuts, Jesse Jackson arguing against Star Wars, a college debater attempting to prove that capital punishment is desirable, and a student senate leader trying to convince fellow students that the student senate is doing a good job are all cases of persuasion to convince.

Because speeches to convince appeal to the listener's intelligence rather than emotions, they employ logical rather than psychological or personal appeals. They must rely on clear reasoning and carefully selected evidence in order to get listeners to respond satisfactorily. Six forms of supporting evidence: examples, explanation, statistics, testimony, comparison/contrast, and visual aids were presented in detail in chapter 4 under supporting devices. A review of chapter 4 should help you develop the speech to convince.

Speeches to Reinforce

Rather than appealing to their intelligence, a speech to reinforce appeals essentially to the motives, attitudes, and sentiments of an audience. Rather than being undecided, indifferent, or opposed, the audience is in agreement with the speaker's point of view.

On Veterans Day a speaker reminds the audience of the sacrifices made by those who fought and died so that each of them might enjoy this land of freedom. Those in the audience already believe that the sacrifices made by these veterans were important. However, the speaker wants to strengthen that belief, to reinforce that appreciation, to deepen that concern.

The Independence Day orator, the speaker at a pep rally, the commencement speaker, the preacher, and the persons delivering eulogies, inaugural addresses, memorials, and testimonials are involved with persuasion to reinforce. Their purpose is to strengthen the existing attitudes, sentiments, emotions, and beliefs of their audience.

Speeches to Actuate

The speech to actuate calls for a specific action on the part of the audience. It asks them to buy, to join, to march, to sign. A speech to convince may attempt to create an awareness in the audience as to the danger to our society caused by easy access to handguns; the speech to actuate seeks to get those in the audience to write to their representatives in congress urging them to vote to get handguns off the streets. A speech to reinforce may seek to arouse greater concern for the plight of the hungry in our society; the speech to actuate would seek an overt response asking the audience for a specific donation of food or money to respond directly to the problem.

While the speech to actuate may employ the logical and psychological appeals used in speeches to convince and reinforce, the purpose of this speech is to get specific action. For this reason, speeches to actuate are generally more successful when directed at audiences that basically agree with the persuader's point of view.

SAMPLE SPEECH AND COMMENTARY

Below is the text and commentary of a persuasive speech delivered by a student in a public speaking class at the Milwaukee Area Technical College. It provides a clear model of a speech to actuate.

SAMPLE SPEECH TO ACTUATE

Do Yourself a Favor: Jog

(See commentary on pages 135–136)

1. *Introduction.* When I first came to this school, I was out of shape physically, about twenty pounds overweight, and emotionally depressed. Now, six months later, I realize that all three of my problems had the same cause: I wasn't exercising enough. It wasn't that I hadn't tried. I had tried racquetball, softball, volleyball, and tennis. I didn't stay with any of them. Part of the problem was that with each of these activities, I had to set aside regular hours, but my schedule changed from day to day. Then one day, I picked up a copy of Jim Fixx's book on running, and I began considering jogging as an exercise. I read a few more books on jogging and found that it has some definite benefits: (1) it strengthens the heart, (2) it aids in removing unwanted fat, and (3) it develops good emotional balance. Another advantage for me was that a person can jog at any time, day or night. It sounded like a good exercise, so I started to jog. I have been jogging now for six months, and I see it as the ideal exercise.

I believe that after you hear what I have to say, you'll want to try jogging, too. Keep in mind that no matter what your age, if you are in good physical condition, you can jog. A child can begin jogging when he or she is old enough to run safely. An adult in good physical condition can jog at virtually any age. I read about one 78-year old man who recently completed the grueling 26-mile San Francisco Marathon. So, if you decide to jog, here is what it will do for you.

2. *Body.* The first benefit I mentioned is that jogging strengthens the heart. The advantage of a strong heart is that it pumps blood more efficiently, working less and resting more. As you can see from this chart, jogging strengthens the heart in four ways: (1) it improves collateral (auxiliary) circulation; (2) it increases the efficiency of the heart in extracting oxygen from the blood; (3) it lowers the fat concentration in the blood; and (4) it lowers blood pressure. These benefits to the heart significantly reduce the risk of heart attack and stroke. A scientific study of the benefits of jogging administered to a group of Harvard graduates indicated that the rate of heart attacks for those who exercised the equivalent of twenty miles of jogging per week was 39 percent below those who exercised lightly or not at all.

Secondly, jogging aids in removing unwanted fat. Whatever extra weight the runner is carrying makes running more difficult. Therefore, the incentive to lose weight increases. Losing weight often improves a person's physical appearance, but, more importantly, it can significantly improve one's health. Dr. Kenneth Cooper, a renowned authority on aerobics, states: ". . . obesity may be a more mysterious killer than many people expect." He estimates that more than 50 million Americans are seriously obese, collectively carrying more than one billion pounds of extra weight. Anyone who is more than 20 percent heavier than his or her ideal weight is considered obese. Getting rid of that extra weight could add years to a person's life, and jogging can help you to accomplish this objective. A recent survey that appeared in *Runners' World* magazine showed that two-thirds of the runners who responded had lost between 10 and 20 pounds through jogging.

Thirdly, jogging develops good emotional balance. Perhaps the most important prerequisite of emotional well-being is a good self-concept. In her book, "The Psychic Power of Running," Valerie Andrews calls jogging "the ultimate exercise and man's healthiest activity." She says that jogging combines the achievement of physical fitness with the satisfaction of self-actualization. A jogger almost always experiences a boost in self-confidence due to his or her improved physical condition. This is often accomplished by a feeling of fulfillment and self-worth. The emotional benefits of jogging are well-documented. A controlled experiment at the University of Wisconsion by Dr. John Greist found jogging far superior to psychotherapy as a treatment for patients with clinical depression. This coincides with a view widely accepted among psychologists and psychiatrists who see this exercise resulting in lowered levels of depression and anxiety.

3. *Conclusion.* As you have heard, the benefits of jogging are impressive. The fact that it strengthens the heart, lessening the risk of heart attack, stroke, and heart disease could prolong your life. The emotional balance it provides will help to reduce your anxiety and increase your ability to handle stress. Finally, the fact that it aids in reducing unwanted fat will improve both your health and appearance. These are all good reasons for starting this ideal exercise. So, pick up a book on jogging and follow the instructions, get approval from your physician if you are in doubt about your physical condition, and start jogging.

Bibliography

ANDREWS, VALERIE, *The Psychic Power of Running.* New York: Ballantine Books, 1979.

COOPER, KENNETH, *The Aerobics Program for Total Well-Being.* New York: M. Evans and Company, Inc., 1982.

"Dietary Habits of Runners," in *The Complete Runner*, eds. of Runners World Magazine. New York: Avon, 1978.

FIXX, JIM, *Jim Fixx's Second Book of Running.* New York: Random House, 1980.

MIRKIN, GABE and MARSHALL HOFFMAN, *The Sportsmedicine Book.* Boston: Little, Brown and Company, 1978.

MORGAN, WILLIAM P., "The Mind of a Marathoner," *Psychology Today*, April 1978, pp. 43–46.

Source: Used with permission of the speaker, Kai Koch

Commentary

In the introduction, the speaker introduces the deductive premise that people who are out of shape, overweight, and depressed have problems. He gains credibility by establishing a common bond with his listeners as a fellow student and indicating to them that he has read a number of books on jogging. He then introduces three inductive premises: (1) jogging strengthens the heart, (2) it aids in removing unwanted fat, and (3) it develops good emotional balance. These premises lead to the conclusion that jogging is the ideal exercise. Listing these premises also previews the main points to be covered in the speech. Finally, the speaker indicates that the purpose of the speech is to persuade the audience to try jogging as an exercise.

In the first body paragraph, the speaker uses explanation, visual aids, testimony, statistics, and comparison to support the premise that jogging strengthens the heart. The speaker appeals to the listener's motive of security in pointing out that the risk of heart attack is much less for those who jog twenty miles or more per week.

In the second body paragraph, the speaker appeals to the listener's motives of approval, popularity, and security. Losing weight will make you look better and avoid the danger of the "mysterious killer," obesity. He uses explanation, testimony, example, and statistics to support the premise that jogging aids in removing unwanted fat.

In the third body paragraph, the speaker appeals to the listener's motives of approval, success, and security by pointing out that jogging improves self-concept and promotes self-actualization by making a person more physically fit and less anxious or depressed. He uses testimony, explanation, statistics, and comparison to support the premise that jogging develops good emotional balance.

In the conclusion, the speaker uses the techniques of summary and restatement to remind the audience of the main points of the speech and its central idea. He then ends with a call for action from the audience.

EXERCISES

Speaking Assignments

1. *Persuasion to reinforce.* Develop a three-to-four-minute speech to reinforce. Remember, persuasion to reinforce is directed at an audience that already agrees with you. You are seeking to make that agreement stronger. Rely chiefly on psychological proof. Appeal to your audience's motives, attitudes, and sentiments.

Delivery: The speech to reinforce seeks to strengthen the audience's beliefs. It is imperative that they feel the speaker is sincere. The more relaxed and spontaneous you are, the more likely it will be that you will succeed.

SAMPLE CENTRAL IDEAS

1. We are all unique.
2. You can make a difference.
3. We owe senior citizens a lot.
4. Be proud of our flag.

2. *Persuasion to convince.* Develop a three-to-four-minute speech supporting a point of view you feel many in your audience are either undecided about or are against. Appeal to your audience's intelligence. Present your material objectively and fairly. An audience will react negatively to a speaker they perceive as being biased.

SUGGESTIONS

1. Try to establish a common bond with your audience.
2. Try to show your listeners that your motives are sincere.
3. Don't attempt too much in this assignment. If you can get those in your audience to modify their views even slightly, you will have been effective.

SAMPLE CENTRAL IDEAS

1. The U.S. should adopt a system of socialized medicine.
2. The U.S. government should prohibit the sale of handguns.
3. The death penalty should be reestablished (abolished) in our state.
4. Our military budget should be reduced by one-third.

3. *Persuasion to actuate.* Develop a two-to-three-minute speech to persuade your audience to act in a particular way. Make clear to your audience exactly what you want them to do. Remember, you are asking your audience to act: to sign, to vote, to buy, to march, to donate, or to participate. Be realistic. Don't ask them to do something they are unlikely to do.

SAMPLE CENTRAL IDEAS

1. Begin an exercise program.
2. Do a fire check of your home.
3. Hug a loved one today.
4. Don't use loaded words.

chapter eleven

GROUP
COMMUNICATION

If you are like most people, you participate in some form of group discussion almost daily. There are all kinds of group discussions. They may be planned or spontaneous, structured or unstructured, formal or informal, permanent or temporary. Some discussions take place with a group of friends over coffee or with fellow workers during the lunch hour. Others occur in the home where everything from the high cost of living to what to do about the neighbor's dog may be covered. More and more, however, discussions are occurring more formally in organized committees and action groups.

During the last few years citizens have become increasingly involved in the affairs of their communities. Organizations like MADD (Mothers Against Drunk Driving) and CUB (Citizens' Utility Board) have sprung up as a result of people demanding to have a voice in determining policies that affect their lives.

Discussions are also a vital part of formal education. Many instructors employ a lecture-discussion format, and group discussion is often used in classes to promote learning. The advantages of your becoming a more effective participant in discussion are obvious. A study of the principles of group discussion, together with guided practice, will help you achieve this goal.

THE FUNCTIONS OF DISCUSSION

In general, discussion has four functions: social, therapeutic, educative, and problem solving.

Social Discussion

Social discussion usually occurs spontaneously and is temporary, unstructured, and informal. A typical example of social discussion would be a group of students sitting around a table in the student union discussing federal budget cuts in aid-to-education programs. Another example might be a group of businessmen discussing federal budget cuts from an entirely different viewpoint over cocktails at the nineteenth hole of the local country club. Neither group will resolve the problem they are discussing. However, many of the participants will benefit from the interchange of ideas, the reinforcement of attitudes, and the enjoyment that social discussion groups provide.

Educative Discussion

The function of educative discussion (sometimes called information-seeking discussion) is to make you better informed about the topic discussed. Examples of educative discussion groups include garden clubs, Bible study groups, musical societies, and book clubs. One of the most familiar examples of educative discussion is classroom discussion, which is particularly well suited to the speech class. A brief discussion following each classroom speech can provide valuable feedback to both the speaker and the audience. An all-class discussion of the textbook and the exams will help students better understand speech principles and what is expected of them.

Therapeutic Discussion

A second type of discussion group is the therapeutic group. The leader of this type is almost always a trained therapist, whose goal is the personal improvement of each member. Examples of therapeutic groups include alcohol and drug rehabilitation groups, marriage-counseling groups, religious encounter groups, and weight-watching groups. These provide a supportive atmosphere where individuals can learn why they act the way they do and what they can do to change their behavior.

Problem-Solving Discussion

Group problem solving is superior to individual problem solving for a number of reasons. First, an individual's background and experience can seldom match those of a group. The more people there are working on a problem, the more information there is available to solve it. Second, the more people you have looking at a problem, the more likely you are able to solve it correctly. In a group an error by one individual is likely to be spotted by someone else.

As our society grows increasingly complex, more and more problems that must be dealt with are surfacing. The majority of them will be addressed in problem-solving group discussion. In governmental committee meetings, business conferences, church councils, legislative sessions, classroom meetings, and the like, problems are being solved, policies are being determined, and decisions are being made that affect the lives of millions of people. As an educated person, you will be called upon to participate in a variety of discussion situations. A study of the principles of group communication, together with guided practice, will help you to develop the knowledge and skill necessary for effective participation.

TYPES OF DISCUSSION

Since the discussion groups you participate in will most likely be either educative or problem solving, the rest of this chapter will concentrate only on these. The five basic types of discussion are the round table, the panel, the symposium, the lecture forum, and the dialogue.

The Round Table

In the round table discussion the participants sit at a round table or in a circle. There are two reasons for this seating arrangement: (1) when seated in a circle, everyone is in a position to maintain eye contact with the others while speaking or listening to them, and (2) no one is seated in a superior "head of the table" position. Each participant is in a position equal to that of his or her neighbor. Everyone, including the moderator or leader if there is one, is involved in a round table discussion. There is no audience. This type of discussion is particularly suited to council and committee meetings, conferences, and classroom discussions. Although round table discussions usually involve from three to fifteen members, an effective classroom discussion can be held with as many as twenty-five.

The Panel

A panel usually consists of from three to six panelists and a moderator. The members sit in front of an audience or judge in a circle or semicircle so that they can see and react to each other. The language used by panel members is usually informal and conversational. Although panel participants are often made aware of the discussion problem beforehand, most panels are unrehearsed to insure spontaneity and enthusiasm during the presentation.

Panels that are followed by an audience participation period, or forum, are usually timed. For example, for a one-hour program, forty minutes might be set aside for the panel and twenty minutes for the forum period. It is the moderator's job to summarize the discussion and field the questions from the audience.

The Symposium

Unlike round table and panel discussions, which are like magnified conversations, the symposium consists of a series of prepared speeches, each dealing with a specific aspect of the same topic. The number of speakers for a symposium usually ranges from three to five. A time limit is given to each of the speakers, who talk directly to the audience rather than to each other. The moderator opens the discussion, introduces each speaker and topic, and summarizes the discussion at the conclusion. If there is a forum period following the summary, the moderater fields the questions, rephrasing them when necessary.

The Lecture Forum

The lecture forum involves a moderator and a lecturer, who delivers a prepared speech on a subject. The speech is followed by a forum period. The job of the moderator is to introduce the subject and speaker and preside during the forum period. The lecture-forum technique has long been used by classroom teachers and political candidates, who then field questions from the audience.

Another variation of the lecture forum is the film forum. The success of this technique is largely dependent on the quality of the film shown and the ability of the moderator to deal effectively with any questions the audience may have regarding the film.

The Dialogue

A dialogue is an interchange and discussion of ideas between two people. It is highly successful when both participants know their subjects well. The dialogue can be a useful classroom exercise. It is an excellent means of communicating information. For best results, the dialogue should be carefully planned so that both participants know where the discussion is heading.

PARTICIPATING IN DISCUSSION

To a great extent, successful discussion depends on the participants. Sometimes discussions fail because the participants have little knowledge of the subject and, consequently, little to offer in solving the problem. At other times a discussion ends in aimless argument because of the inflexibility or refusal to compromise. Breakdowns in communication, an unfriendly atmosphere, and a tendency to stray from the subject also contribute to the failure of discussion. Effective participation in discussion requires both ability and understanding. Following are the duties of a discussion:

Listen Carefully

Critical listening is essential to effective discussion. It is an active process requiring both attention and concentration. All too often discussants respond to what they "thought" someone meant. If you are unclear as to the meaning of something that was said during a discussion, say so before the discussion continues.

Be Prepared

Every member of a discussion has a responsibility to be well informed on the topic being discussed. This means that if you have little knowledge of the subject, you spend time and effort researching it. If you are delivering a lecture or are a member of a symposium panel, prepare and practice your speech carefully so that you can deliver it extemporaneously with good eye contact.

Be Spontaneous

Participate whenever you have something relevant to say. Although you must not interrupt another speaker, if you have something important to say, interject it when there is a pause in the conversation. A relevant comment in the right place can often save the group time.

Share the Spotlight

Although you should participate when you have a worthwhile contribution, don't monopolize the discussion. Group thinking can be thought of as thinking out loud. Unless all members contribute, the full value of their knowledge and experience will not be brought to bear upon the problem.

Be Friendly

The old saying "You catch more flies with honey than with vinegar" is especially appropriate to the group discussion situation. Group discussion requires flexibility and compromise. It is unlikely that either will occur in a hostile atmosphere.

Be Cooperative

Participants in group discussion must put the best interests of the group above their own personal interests. The goal of discussion is to arrive at a solution acceptable to all members of the group. This means that group members must be willing to work cooperatively to avoid conflict.

Be Objective

In order for a discussion to be successful each member must approach the question in an unbiased, objective way. If for some reason you have a strongly held attitude that would prevent you from discussing a topic objectively, excuse yourself from the discussion group.

Stick to the Point

Few things are more frustrating to a group than when a member introduces material that is completely off the subject. It is every member's responsibility to keep the discussion on track. Always be aware of where the discussion is heading and contribute only when your remarks are pertinent.

Use Time Wisely

A discussion participant should avoid belaboring a point. Once agreement is reached in regard to some aspect of the problem, it is time to move on. To explain to the group why you made the same decision as another member is counterproductive.

Speak Clearly

Unless the listener understands the message, communication does not take place. If you want to be understood, be careful to articulate your words carefully and pronounce them correctly. Speak with adequate volume and emphasize important points so that the other members of the group know exactly where you stand.

Be Natural

No matter which form of discussion you are involved in, be yourself. Speak in a conversational manner. An advantage to using a conversational style is that you will feel comfortable with it. If you try to change your way of speaking, you are liable to sound stilted and unnatural.

MODERATING THE DISCUSSION

Most discussion forms require a moderator. Seven specific duties of a moderator are listed here:

1. Start the discussion by introducing the topic and the lecturer or discussion participants to the audience.
2. Direct the discussion by seeing to it that the subject is adequately discussed and that the group moves steadily toward a solution or conclusion.
3. Encourage participation. Members who do not take part in the discussion contribute little or nothing to the outcome.
4. Resolve conflicts by using tact and diplomacy to minimize tension.
5. Control the time to make sure all aspects of the problem are discussed.
6. Provide transitions and summaries to help participants see what has been accomplished and what remains to be done.
7. Take charge of the forum period. Field all questions, rephrasing when necessary.

A PATTERN FOR PROBLEM SOLVING

Identifying the Problem

The first step in problem-solving discussion is to have the members pinpoint the problem. Many discussions fail because the problem is not clearly understood by all. Next, the problem must be carefully worded. When wording the problem for discussion, the group should adhere to the following guidelines:

1. The problem should be worded in the form of a question. A properly worded question holds up a problem in such a way as to motivate discussants to seek solutions to it.

2. It should be phrased to avoid a yes or no answer. Participants who answer yes or no to a question often feel committed to defend that answer. The result is that what started out as objective discussion turns into subjective debate.

3. It should be stated in an impartial way. A discussion question should never indicate bias. The question, When will we stop the stupid sale of hand guns? is prejudiced. It would be far better to ask, How can the sale of hand guns be effectively regulated?

4. It should be worded specifically. The question, What should the government do to prevent terrorism? is far too vague. Which government are we talking about? Where will the terrorism take place? A better question would be, What steps should the federal government take to prevent terrorists from illegally entering the United States?

5. It should be sufficiently restricted. The question, What should be done to stop world hunger? is so broad that it could not be adequately covered in a set period of time. A better question would be, What should be done to stop hunger in the United States?

Analyzing the Problem

After identifying and wording the problem, the nature and causes of the problem should be explored. The group should consider such questions as these: What is the history of the problem? How serious is it? Who is affected by it? What are the causes?

The process of analysis usually requires research. Participants should research the discussion problem just as they would research the topic for a speech. A thorough investigation of the problem will give discussants a clear understanding of what conditions need correcting.

The final step in analysis is to decide on guidelines to evaluate proposed solutions. These guidelines should be agreed upon before possible solutions are proposed. A typical list of guidelines might include: It must be safe; it must be affordable; it must be obtainable; and it must not create new problems.

Finding the Best Solution

At this point members of the group should suggest possible solutions. It is a good idea to identify as many solutions as possible before evaluating any of them. An effective way to compile an adequate list of solutions is by using a technique called brainstorming.

In a discussion the brainstorming technique can be handled in two ways. The first is to have members of the group write down whatever solutions that come to mind as quickly as they can. They should jot them down in phrases or sentences without evaluating them. After five minutes the exercise stops, and each list of solutions is read aloud. The second technique has one member of the group proposing a solution, another posing a different one, and so on. The brainstorming continues for a set period of time or until the group has no more solutions to offer. One member should be assigned to write down all the ideas.

Once a list of solutions has been established, the group can quickly eliminate any that are illogical or repetitive. The remaining solutions can then be evaluated according to the guidelines established earlier. It is wise for the group to evaluate each solution on the list before making their choice.

Finally, the group should make every effort to reach agreement as to the best solution or solutions. If they cannot reach a consensus, a majority vote should be taken.

Actuating the Solution

Once the group has agreed on a solution, it is necessary to take action. This might mean drafting a letter and sending it to the appropriate representatives in Washington, framing a petition and collecting signatures, or planning and staffing a fund-raising event. Perhaps the proposed solution will take the form of an oral report to the mayor and city council or to your instructor and the rest of the class. Sometimes a solution will require a written report. Whatever action is taken, the last job the group has is to implement the solution it chooses.

USING CASE PROBLEMS

The best way to develop ability in group discussion is through guided practice. The use of case problems as discussion questions is an effective way of stimulating this practice. These problems are typical of those that occur in everyday life and are the kinds of situations you are likely to encounter at school, at work, or at home.

There are no "right" or "wrong" solutions to these problems. However, each problem is constructed in such a way that choosing a solution poses a dilemma. For each problem there are two alternative solutions, both of which are undesirable. The job of the group is to choose the solution they see as being the least undesirable.

Remember, the group should make an effort to reach agreement on a solution for each problem. If they cannot reach a consensus, the solution should be chosen by majority opinion.

EVALUATING DISCUSSIONS

The discussion rating form shown in figure 11-1 is designed for both student and instructor evaluation. It lists the characteristics to be considered when evaluating a discussion.

DISCUSSION RATING FORM

Scale: 1 superior, 2 above ave., 3 average, 4 poor

Names: (John M.) (Mary S.) (Robert R.) (George S.)

	Names	(John M.)	(Mary S.)	(Robert R.)	(George S.)
PARTICIPATION—Listened carefully; was prepared; was spontaneous; used pertinent information; tested the thinking of others.					
ATTITUDE—Was friendly; tactful; cooperative; flexible; objective.					
THOUGHT PROGRESSION—Spoke to the point; stayed on the subject; used time wisely.					
COMMUNICATIVE SKILLS—Used adequate volume; was clear, was conversational; observed the rules of grammar.					

OVERALL RATING FOR GROUP _____

COMMENTS:

FIGURE 11-1   DISCUSSION RATING FORM

EXERCISES

Case Problems[1]

1. Mary F., who works at a sewing factory, ran a sewing-machine needle through her finger. As superintendent of the factory, you sent her to the company doctor. He declared it was a clean wound and sent her back to work without giving her a tetanus shot as a precaution against lockjaw. The company is responsible for payment of all expenses incurred by a worker in connection with a job-connected injury.

What should you do?

2. A foreman is suspicious that one of his workers is connected with the Communist party and may eventually influence other workers. The suspected employee, however, is respected by his fellow workers and popular with them. He is competent and efficient at his job.

In this situation what, if anything, should the foreman do?

3. You are a production foreman in an automotive-parts fabricating plant. Company policy regarding credit given for employees' suggestions is to reward the first person who turns in a useful suggestion in written form. John has developed an idea concerning a manufacturing problem. He is ready to write it and turn it in, but George, a second employee, learns of the idea and turns in the written suggestion before John. As the foreman, these facts are known to you. Because the idea is a very useful one, you should reward one of the employees.

What should you do?

4. You, a senior, have noticed that a sophomore, whom you know well and who works near you in the physics laboratory, often slips small pieces of equipment into his pocket and carries them away from the laboratory. You have never seen him return any of these items. Some of the pieces are of considerable value and you suspect that he is either selling them or using them to equip a small laboratory of his own.

What should you do?

5. A few days before the final examination you learn by chance that another student in one of your courses has a copy of the questions to be used on the test and that he is passing it among his friends in the course. You know that several students in the course have already seen it and you suspect that nearly a third of those in the course have seen it.

What should you do?

Source: Problems 1–5 are used with permission of the author from William E. Utterback, *Group Thinking and Conference Leadership*, rev. ed. (New York: Holt, Rinehart and Winston, Inc., 1964). Problems 6–17 have been taken with permission from Arthur Koch and Stanley B. Felber, *What Did You Say?* 3rd ed. (Englewood Cliffs, N.J.: Prentice-Hall, 1985).

6. Fred and John, close personal friends, work together part time stocking shelves at a local supermarket. Fred has been working to buy himself a new car while John has taken the second job to help support a widowed mother and nine brothers and sisters. One night after closing time Fred notices John carrying a case of powdered milk out to his car.
What should Fred do?

7. John, a white student at a small out-of-state technical college, has fallen in love with Cindy, a black student at the same school. He plans to invite her home for Christmas, but he does not plan to tell his parents beforehand that she is black. He argues that his parents have always insisted that they were unprejudiced, and now he will be able to see by their reaction if they are honest. Cindy does not agree.
How should the situation be handled?

8. Joan and Donna have been friends since childhood. Lately, Donna has been seeing a lot of an older, married man. Joan advises Donna to break this off, but Donna is convinced that the man plans to get a divorce and marry her. Donna has told her parents that she will be visiting Joan for the weekend so that she and the man can go off together.
What should Joan do?

9. Upon your college roommate's return from summer vacation he tells you he is engaged. When he shows you his fiancée's picture, you recognize her as a former classmate who has a reputation for being promiscuous. You like your roommate very much.
What should you do?

10. When visiting his friend Ralph for the weekend, Carl sees him take ten dollars from his mother's purse. On the following day Carl is present as the mother accuses Ralph's brother Tim of stealing the money. She punishes Tim by taking away his use of the car for two months.
What should Carl do?

11. While you are riding home with Sue, a good friend, she backs into a parked car, causing considerable damage. Although she has liability insurance, she refuses to leave her name, explaining that she has already had two accidents this year and is afraid that her insurance policy will be cancelled. Sue drives a total of fifty miles to and from school every day.
What should you do?

12. Julia is engaged to be married to Fred. The wedding is less than two months away, and Fred suggests that they begin their sexual relationship so that they can be sure that there are no physical or psychological barriers to a happy marriage. Julia believes very strongly that she should remain chaste before the wedding. Fred insists.
What should Julia do?

13. In 1966 John Graff was sentenced to life imprisonment for the murder of his business partner, Harry Fosdick. During his trial and imprisonment Graff had protested his innocence. He was released in April 1986 after serving the full twenty years at Joliet prison in Illinois and returned to Chicago, his hometown. Two days later he ran into Fosdick, the man he had been convicted of murdering. At this meeting, in the presence of witnesses, Fosdick admitted that he had intentionally framed Graff. The following day Fosdick was found murdered. When arrested for the crime, Graff admitted his guilt but claimed he was temporarily insane at the time. What punishment, if any, should Graff get?

14. Henry, a rookie police officer, has been assigned to the vice squad temporarily to do undercover work. His job, for which he has grown a full beard, is to uncover prostitution. During his first night on the job he is propositioned by a woman he recognizes as the wife of a fellow police officer. Because of the beard she does not recognize him. What should he do?

15. Penny Smith, a white coed, worked as a volunteer staff person for the political campaign of Wanda Jones, a young, idealistic black woman. Wanda ran against George Alport, a member of the American Nazi party. Wanda won a narrow victory, which Penny, through involvement in the campaign, can prove was the result of voter fraud. What should Penny do?

16. Sally and Bess have been best friends since childhood. Recently Bess has started a new job working in an office with Sally's husband Sam. She soon learns that Sam is having an affair with one of the secretaries. Bess believes that if Sally finds out it will destroy her marriage. What should Bess do?

17. Fred's fifteen-year-old daughter, Ann, has recently begun a part-time job babysitting with his employer's young children. After her second night on the job she confides to Fred that the children have told her they are often beaten by their father. She says she has seen the marks of this abuse. She feels that the authorities should be notified. Fred is concerned about losing his job. What should Fred do?

INDEX